MERYL PUGH

Meryl Pugh lives in East London and holds a PhD in Critical and Creative Writing from the University of East Anglia. She teaches creative writing, most recently as a lecturer at UEA. She is the author of three pamphlets and one collection of poetry. *Natural Phenomena* (2018) was a Poetry Book Society Guest Choice and longlisted for the Laurel Prize.

OLIVER BARRETT (ILLUSTRATOR)

Oliver Barrett is a musician and illustrator based in Somerset. He releases music under his own name, Petrels, Sun Do Silver, Glottalstop, Sphagnum Moss, and many more besides. His first, self-illustrated book, *The Nuckelavee*, was published by Tartaruga Press in 2015. You can see more of his work at floatinglimb.com

ALSO BY MERYL PUGH

Feral Borough

Meryl Pugh

with illustrations by Oliver Barrett

Penned in the Margins
LONDON

PUBLISHED BY PENNED IN THE MARGINS
Toynbee Studios, 28 Commercial Street, London E1 6AB
www.pennedinthemargins.co.uk

First published in 2022

Printed and bound in the United Kingdom by TJ Books Limited.

ISBN
978-1-908058-95-9

CONTENTS

In memory of

DONALD EDWARD PUGH
1940 – 2018

TARA LOUISE FEW
1968 – 2013

§

and for Richard

Feral Borough

Common Buzzard

Buteo buteo

It is April and the neighbours' children are playing in the garden. One of them has managed to turn on the sprinkler – much commotion as their mum admonishes Grandad, who is supposed to be supervising them. The children hoot with excitement while the sprinkler is turned off and a towel is fetched. The littlest one has learnt to say *water*.

A kerfuffle of pigeons, as if to mirror the human kerfuffle. Then a crow giving a half-strangled 'kark'. I look up – and it's harrying a – what? Bigger than the crow, brown, those big wings with the slightly blunt taper at the end – yes, maybe, is it? A buzzard, veering, jinking, dipping from the crow's aim, crossing over to the Flats.

Later, I check on the London Birders' Wiki page. There it is, recorded. *Buteo buteo.*

It is the end of June, a year after my buzzard sighting, and we are having another short run of fine days. England is in lockdown (SARS-CoV-2 made landfall a few months ago) and excited children's voices draw me to the front room window. The neighbours and their kids are out in the street. The eldest child tiptoes to place a hand on a car window, while her mother carries her little brother on her hip. Their grandfather is in the car, all the windows closed, trying to make himself audible as he chats with his daughter. The little girl shouts to him and he aligns his hand with hers, the other side of the glass.

Without so much of the pollution haze, the sky seems a prism in which every one of its inhabitants is sharp against the blue. High up, in wide, slow circles, with hardly any wingbeats, the wings that look like butter knives twisted and damaged at the end or, no, like fish knives. A gull describes smaller circles, then veers and dips in attack threats that don't impact.

The wide circling carries on. Beauty, oh beauty, oh.

Feral Pigeon
Columba livia domestica

It is May and very hot – *unseasonal* is the word that everyone uses. I am sitting beside a pond in a park near Waterloo, eating a sandwich before I teach my evening class. Feral pigeons are milling around, purring and bowing and puffing up their breast feathers at each other or stalking jerkily towards any remnants of dropped food. I stare at the water, wishing I was brave enough to dunk my feet. There is a clapping noise as the birds skirl into the air. One passes so close to me that I feel the small wind raised by its wings on my cheek. What happens next astounds me.

Pigeons are taking turns to fly into the pond, flapping furiously to hover above, then letting their bodies touch the surface of the water as they dip and ruffle first the head into the water, then the breast, then wings, before they rise with strong, fast wingbeats to land on the bank.

Then one actually settles on the water, like a duck. Its wings spread out in a wide spatula shape to help it float as it dips its head, wets its whole self. I have never seen anything like it before.

When I moved into this house – the one in which I'm writing this book – I didn't pay much attention to its wildlife or landscape. In fact, *wildlife* and *landscape* both seemed redundant words for my new home and its surroundings. We moved here in the late nineties, leaving behind our flat in North West London to settle on the opposite side of the A-to-Z in Leytonstone. Housing was – for London – relatively cheap, the transport links were many and various, our workplaces half an hour away by Tube. The house was on a quiet, tree-lined road and had a small garden; we loved it the minute we saw it. But as for nature and wildlife? It didn't have much of that. We were closer to the city, deeper in; there didn't seem to be much room for the wild. I didn't count the tree outside the house as 'nature' back then, nor the feral pigeons squatting outside the Tube station.

I was wrong, of course. As I got to know the area better, I realised that the constant noise from the motorway that cuts it in half, the congested local roads, the rows of terraced houses and blocks of flats; these are only part of the story. Shepherd's purse between a lamppost and the tarmac. Herb robert between a shopfront and the pavement. Those feral pigeons. Foxes.

Leytonstone is part of the London Borough of Waltham Forest, one of the 'new' boroughs created in 1965, when Greater London's boundaries were redrawn. Before this, it was considered a a subsidiary part of the Leyton district in the county of Essex. The name Leyton-atte-Stone originally designated a small number of dwellings that stood near a milestone on the eastbound road. In his history of the area, the wonderfully named W. G. Hammock notes that in 1584, 'Leytonstone was then only a dependent hamlet' of Leyton and quotes David John Morgan, a former Conservative MP for Walthamstow and Councillor for Leytonstone, who recalls that it was 'one of the prettiest villages which could be imagined.' In his younger days, Morgan would walk

> ... [f]rom the Church northwards ... passing what was then a field ... Mr. Payze's farmyard, straw-littered, with its large black gate and black thatched barn, and then, beyond, a number of cottages with gardens which were always bright with flowers.

Then came the speculative building boom in the latter half of the nineteenth century and the village was swallowed up.

Poverty and wealth exist cheek-by-jowl in present-day Leytonstone, just as in the rest of London. Bookmakers and charity shops proliferate on the high street and one of the libraries has closed. A food bank operates out of the local church opposite a volunteer-run art gallery, while a nearby pub offers shabby chic sofas and boutique rooms upstairs. The views are of power pylons vaulting over to Ilford in one direction, and in another, above the roofs of Victorian and Edwardian terraces, the tower blocks that were once social housing. Past those, there is the punctuation of the buildings at Canary Wharf, The Shard and other nervy, twenty-first century attempts upon the London skyline.

Leytonstone is surrounded by a lot of green space, sitting as it does at the foot of Epping Forest's insurgence into the city from Essex. Beyond the high street, there is a scrubbily untidy wood with an avenue of trees leading out of it towards a playing field. Further east, in Wanstead, there's a park, formerly the grounds of a gentleman's estate, where the ornamental ponds stink in summer and fill with bread crusts and drinks cans. They also sport kingfishers, herons, gulls, tufted ducks and greylag geese as well as the obligatory mallards, black-headed gulls and Canada geese. There is even a heath, part of an open expanse called 'the Flats' segueing from grass and copse to playing fields and divided into segments by the roads to Forest Gate and Manor Park. Nature here is raggedly alive, part of a landscape that is neither wholly picturesque nor municipal.

In that respect, Leytonstone and the surrounding area might bring to mind the landscapes tramped over by Richard Mabey in *The Unofficial Countryside* or the *Edgelands* explored by Paul Farley and Michael Symmons Roberts. They call such terrains 'the new wild', 'the domain of the feral' – and I recognise that mixture of built and natural, husbanded and neglected in my local area.

If you look at it one way, there's no such thing as 'wild' anymore, now that our planet's biosphere has been so comprehensively affected by human action. We have changed the weather, changed the ozone layer, changed the oceans and seas – and so there is no part of the planet and no living thing that has not been touched by us, even if only indirectly.* If nature is

---

* And now there is this:

> Nanoplastic pollution has been detected in polar regions for the first time, indicating that the tiny particles are now pervasive around the world. [...] Analysis of a core from Greenland's ice cap showed that nanoplastic contamination has been polluting the remote region for at least 50 years. The researchers were also surprised to find that a quarter of the particles were from vehicle tyres.

in a constant state of negotiation with humanity over territory, adapting, as it experiences resurgence in one place whilst being pushed back in another, then that isn't wildness. That's ferality.

Feral. From the Latin *fera*: 'a wild beast'. Since the nineteenth century, it's denoted a lapse from domestication into wildness. Something once tame, no longer. We use it about people, too. And it's borne of disadvantage, some way in which human society and structure conflict with an entity's needs and well-being. I keep thinking of the cat that Farley and Symmons Roberts conjure for us:

> Here, finding shelter in the old ruins and food in the overgrown wasteland outside, cats forget their pet names, swap the lap and sofa for the pile of discarded overalls, or the car seat with its sporty trim.

That feral cat's transitions between wild and domesticated won't have been easy. However attractively the car seat is presented (that 'sporty trim'), it is 'preferred' to a lap and a sofa because its human companions abused or abandoned or neglected it. Still, that cat's freedom – contingent, yes, and difficult – is powerful: it offers a possible way to keep living somewhere, to make 'home' by

---

Damian Carrington, 'Nanoplastic Pollution Found at Both of Earth's Poles for First Time', *The Guardian*, 2022.

usurping or ignoring boundaries.

And by adapting: those pigeons behaving for a moment like waterfowl, treating rooftops like the cliffs their rock dove ancestors inhabited. A feral species alters its behaviour or alters itself, through successive generations, transforming to meet its new circumstances, a changed environment.

Feral is a good word, too, to describe my neighbourhood. Leytonstone itself seems to be all pieces and edges, cut in half by the M11 Link Road and the Central Line, connected by the latter to both the City proper and the woodland of Epping Forest, topped by a massive sunken roundabout (the 'Green Man') where roads from all the compass points converge. Wanstead Flats, where I spend a lot of my time, straddles the London Boroughs of Waltham Forest, Redbridge and Newham – though, as part of Epping Forest, it also comes under the City of London Corporation's management.

This is my feral borough: Leytonstone, Waltham Forest, green spaces transgressing civic lines. But also more than that. It is a kind of borough-by-affinity, too, made by walking and loitering, looking and recording. It can be found in pockets, scattered throughout the city: on the towpath by the Regent's Canal, in the corner of a Bloomsbury square, a cut-through behind a row of shops. Where plants grow, where quietness pools in corners, the feral borough is made; flickering into being around me. And if the city is a haunted place, a palimpsest, then the feral borough is part of what haunts it. Like the desire paths crossing municipal lawns, or the Parish boundaries delineated by Beating the Bounds, it sharpens with each foray. The imagination builds it as much as the physical, and so I make it not just as a walker or a loiterer but as a reader and a watcher, too. Beside me are the writers and texts that have been so important to me – and so are its fauna. They conjure it with me.

And so the feral borough materialises around me as wood pigeons and swifts give voice in a town beside the Severn river, goldfinch and pied wagtails feed at a university campus, a kestrel hovers above a service station carpark on the M40. Every encounter with these familiars is a moment of home and belonging, where my borough breaks its bounds, trespasses the limits of geography, comes roaring up to hold me. It's not surprising its appearances occur at moments of intense emotion or difficulty in my life – for the feral borough is nothing if it isn't also brought into being by emotion.

I started writing about this landscape and its flora and fauna almost as a way to stay in the city – for as the years wore on, London started to tire me out. It was my home, but it seemed to manifest everything wrong with my modern life: too fast, too loud, too crowded, too abrasive, too polluted, too littered, too much. And every day it brought me face-to-face with what we're doing to the environment: the muck-pink film of haze over the horizon, the squirrel turning a still-wrapped Kit Kat between its paws, the burger wrappers caught in the hedge. Because of love and work, I had to find a way to keep living there, but I didn't know how. Weirdly – or perhaps expectedly – it took the death of one of my closest friends, Tara, to make me see what I was missing. In those changed moments that follow a sudden death, my encounters with the world took on a peculiarly charged quality. I took to walking round the local wood, the parks, the heath – and the plants I saw took on what I can only describe as personalities.

And so I met the feral borough – or made it, or dowsed it, or tuned into it, or invoked it, or conjured it – and now I have inscribed it into these pages. When I started this book, I had no idea I would write something so personal. I thought I was writing a work of non-fiction, something easily categorizable under 'nature writing'. But as I wrote myself into connection with the flora and fauna around me, the entries themselves threw out suckers, sprawled over the fences I had put up – and my own life kept getting snagged on the vines. If the book was a beast, it was misnamed, not wanting to sleep in that kind of bed, refusing to stay put in the territory I allotted to it and doing things that sort of beast was not reputed to do. Its parents were definitely from different species. If it was a plant, it had been wind-blown or pigeon-shat far from its starting point.

So you might also think of this book as a series of bulletins wrung from an unreliable reporter by her encounters in this place. Or maybe they are a collection of greetings, in differing moods and ways, to the often unremarkable local wildlife that shares my habitat – and by extension to the common flora and fauna that inhabit Britain. There have been times when I never thought I'd feel at home anywhere nor that I'd ever be able to call myself a local, but here on this street, it seems I've become embedded. All that noticing and writing wasn't just helping me do the work of grieving, it seems. It has also helped me think myself into this place. Home. And so this book celebrates the joy of being and staying local – extremely so, sometimes restricted to the few metres outside the front door, as the pandemic and the English lockdowns of the last couple of years have forced us to be.

I'm writing this while the neighbours clear up in the kitchen after the evening meal and scaffolding announces another loft conversion. To live here is to realise that everything – houses, roads, people – is always in relationship with everything else. Human and non-human alike, enmeshed as we are, we all transform or mount incursions. The dahlias we planted in our tiny garden go rampant and crowd out the tomatoes, hops take root in the grass verge up the road. 'Nature' is everything and everywhere in the city. It's blocked drains and street-wide puddles, black mould on windowsills, TB, asthma, scabies. And coronaviruses. It's raised voices and vomit on the platform, the dark mice at Holborn with the half-tails. It's parakeets and blackbirds, the howl of planes and the bone-drilling imperatives of power saws. It doesn't wholly submit to human regulation, even as it's changed and harmed by what we do, by our coffee cup lids and carrier bags, by the times we hop into the car instead of taking the bus, by the towers we build and the spaces we pave over and the way we don't listen to what's around us – especially not to each other.

I'm not sure how much longer we'll stay in Leytonstone. Jobs again – and the pull of loved ones in other places, the toll the London air takes on my asthmatic lungs. In the meantime, there is the borough. I go outside onto the high street and here we all are: little kids ogling the cakes in the window of Greggs, the men chatting on their way to Mosque. The late sun uplights a triangular cloud in pink as twilight approaches. I look up from the pavement and there are the parakeets, speeding overhead in full squawk.

To live in the feral borough then is to be in kinship with

everything outside my door. Jackdaws on the bus shelter roof. Someone's snuffling dog, straining against the lead. Those feral pigeons – a fitting emblem for this book – following a buzzard over the terraced streets, keeping the predator firmly in view. That counterpoint between the rare and ordinary, wild and domestic and whatever lies between the two is part of what I love about my home. Living here has taught me so much: to be with both nature *and* the city, noise *and* quiet, life *and* death, to hold all that, all at the same time. Because we humans are feral too, and life is brief.

Artificial Tree

Artificialis arbor

By which I don't mean the dishevelled plastic affair shoved into the cupboard under the stairs, but this oblong, metal tower, parked beside the sculpture at the bus station, with seats of attractive wood set into its base on each side and a series of shelves rising to about four metres, jammed with rolls of moss and houseleeks. This is a city tree – or more properly, a CityTree; 'The World's first biotech pollution filter.' It has a water tank and sensors that monitor pollution levels, it can upload the data wirelessly, it can 'quantifiably improve urban air quality'. I've passed it before while running errands; a curious structure parked on a barren island of paving between road and bus park.

    I visit it properly one clear day in late summer, a day when

London's pollution levels are at the top of the scale. We've been advised not to exert ourselves too heavily, especially if we are older or have heart or lung problems. Asthmatics should carry their inhalers. The strong sunshine is reacting with the city's pollution and the lack of wind prevents it from dispersing. When I emerge from the foot tunnel onto the bus concourse, I start to cough; the stink of bus exhaust is palpable. This area around the station is one of the most polluted in Waltham Forest, placed as it is right beside the M11 Link Road, carved through Leytonstone and Wanstead in the late nineties despite the extended protest.*

Ironic, then, that Leytonstone has acquired a paean to its air quality, albeit one written in 1703. Joseph Harris's 'Leighton-Stone-air, a poem. Or a poetical encomium on the excellency of its soil, healthy air, and beauteous situation' was written on the occasion of the founding of a 'Latin boarding school' and makes much of 'Healthy Leighton's Eppen Plain' and the 'Lovely Villa' wherein, presumably, the school will be based. I do not think Harris would praise quite so lavishly the 'Odours of thy Hemisphere' if he were standing in this spot beside the station.

The cyborg tree is not doing well. The moss is tan and

---

* People camped out in trees, the 'micronations' Wanstonia and Munstonia were established and buildings condemned for demolition were occupied. The road was still built, although the 491 survived as a squatted art gallery until the late 2010s. It's now a block of flats.

shredding out of its rolls. Whole blocks are missing from the shelves, exposing the diamond metal grid behind it. There are a few houseleeks in a bottom corner showing some green, but the rest are grey and desiccated.

Street trees have a notoriously difficult time of it. Their roots are strongly curtailed by the severely compacted soil under pavements and tarmac. Above ground, they have to contend not only with random vandalism or accidental car damage, but higher urban temperatures, dog piss, gritting salt and pollution too. When these conditions weaken them, they fall prey to disease and bugs; most have a shorter life expectancy than their non-urban counterparts. And this strange, hybrid creature – part artifice, part organic – seems to be no exception. Houseleeks belong to the genus *Sempervivum* – 'live forever' – but even they are succumbing to conditions.

I take a couple of pictures on my phone, adjust my glasses and huff on my inhaler. Donna Haraway has said that we are all cyborgs – 'chimeras, theorized and fabricated hybrids of machine and organism'. With medication in my system and this device parked on my nose, I fit the bill. One cyborg meeting another, neither of us entirely thriving in the Odours of the Eppen Plain.

Pride of Leyton

Dianthus caryophyllus var. 'Pride of Leyton'

The carnation variety 'Pride of Leyton' is a picotee – that is, a flower with a different colour or shade at its petals' edges, in this case, darker and lighter purple. But 'Pride of Leyton' might not exist any longer.

It first appears on record in 1887, when Henry Headland exhibits it at the annual exhibition of the National Carnation and Picotee Society, Southern Section, receiving a first-class certificate of merit for his 'very promising flower of excellent quality'. Headland, described in the report as a 'surgical instrument maker', is living at the time of the 1891 Census with his wife and children at 82 The Firs, Leyton. His occupation is listed as 'brass finisher'. The family share the residence with Henry's in-laws, two of whom – the father, Richard, and brother-in-law, William, are florists. It's easy to track Henry's life and career through the years; he wins first place at the annual exhibition in 1888 with 'Pride of Leyton' in the 'Picotees, single bloom – light purple edge' class, and second in 'Picotees, single blooms – Light Red edge' with a variety named 'Souvenir of H. Headland', possibly in memory of his own father, also named Henry, a silversmith who died in 1886. In 1894, he withdraws from the National Carnation and Picotee Society's committee – and by 1901 he is working as an electrical engineer. He lives to the age of ninety and sees his son, Henry William, go into the electrical engineering trade as well, moving with his own family to Hainault Road in Leytonstone, less than a quarter of a mile away.

The year that Headland leaves the committee, one Mr Nutt – who has shown blooms in previous years within the same categories – wins first place at the annual exhibition in a single specimen category for 'Pride of Leyton'. Growers were clearly sharing their plants at these shows. But 'Pride of Leyton' itself is harder to track. I can find no mention of it – nor 'Souvenir of H. Headland', for that matter – in the Classification Booklet of the British National Carnation Society, nor in the Royal Horticultural Society's International Dianthus Register. It has slipped from view.

Did it prove less reliable than hoped? Was it abandoned? Did it hybridize with another variety? There is record of Dianthus 'London Lovely' and Dianthus 'London Brocade', Dianthus 'London Joy' and Dianthus 'London Delight'. There is Dianthus 'London Poppet'. There is Dianthus 'Suffolk Pride' and Dianthus 'Devon Pride' and Dianthus 'Cannup's Pride'. There is even 'London Pride'; an old name from before the eighteenth century for Dianthus barbatus (Sweet William), though it's now applied to *Saxifraga* × *urbium*. But 'Pride of Leyton' has vanished. It is a ghost plant. I can't trace its lineage, can't find its descendants. It only exists in paper and record, tucked away digitally, haunting archival glades.

Somewhere, in these two or so miles, there's a piece of land that retains the footprint of a shed or greenhouse where 'Pride of Leyton' was bred. Maybe there's a trace of that vanished picotee dug into the soil. For under these acres that have been paved over and on which our houses have been built, are other gardens, ghost gardens, entire ghost nurseries.

Leytonstone and the surrounding area was a place for gardeners and horticulture until remarkably late in its history. At Mr Headland's time, it is undergoing the rapid change that transforms it into a London suburb proper. The city is fast encroaching: market gardener James Sweet, for example, has to leave Leyton 'on account [...] of the increase of smoke.' Nevertheless, at the turn of the century, Leytonstone is still the site of several nurseries and market gardening enterprises. There is the 'American Nursery' on Grove Green Road, known for its fine collection of trees, that passed through several hands to horticultural auctioneers Protheroe and Morris, who had already established nurseries in the area. There is the Wallwood Road nursery, run by John Ward who started out as a gardener for the local wealthy, growing orchids amongst other things, before buying an acre of ground in Leytonstone and going into business with his sons: 'the entire acre was soon covered with glass.' In 1901, Leytonstone alone harbours 217 male and 20 female 'gardeners (not domestic), nurserymen, seedsmen, and florists'.

And its history as a centre for botany and horticulture goes still further back. Only four miles away is the estate inherited in 1742 by Richard Warner, a lawyer born into a banking family, who promptly turned it into a botanical garden. A portrait made by Francis Milner Newton in 1755 shows a round, satisfied-looking man with a long, straight nose, one hand tucked between the front buttons of his waistcoat and resting on his stomach. This is the man who imported a new variety of grape from Hamburg in 1726 and played a part in naming a gardenia (*Gardenia jasminoides* J. Ellis). The author of the 1771 work, *Plantae Woodfordienses: A Catalogue of Less Perfect Plants Growing Spontaneously about Woodford in the County of Essex*. A man of consequence.

The gardenia reached the United Kingdom as so many species did, via one of the primary instruments of Britain's colonisation project, the East India Company (another was the Royal African Company, with its trade in enslaved peoples, in which Josiah Child of Wanstead House was involved). The plant was transported between different islands colonised by the Dutch; when they established a supply station at the Cape of what is now South Africa in 1652, they brought it with them. The year before Warner's portrait was completed, Captain William Hutchinson arrived at the Dutch East India Company's colony there, encountered the plant and brought it back to England, where he gave it to Richard Warner, who became a director of the Company six years later. The gardenia survived its voyage, flowered in Warner's hothouse and drew great interest, notable as it was for the strong scent that earnt its comparison with jasmine (hence *jasminoides* in its scientific name).

In the history of my own borough's entanglement with botany, this narrative is repeated again and again. To adapt Ambalavaner Sivanandan's memorable formulation, they are here because we were there. So, enter Gilbert Slater of Low Leyton, director of the East India Company and owner in 1758 of the *Richmond* – a privateer ship with 22 guns on board – and between 1787 and 1793, the *Carnatic* – an 'East Indiaman' merchant ship with 26 guns. It was aboard the *Carnatic* that Captain John Corner brought two varieties of camellia for Slater, the first to arrive in England; *Camellia japonica* 'Alba Plena', a white camellia with double flowers, and *Camellia japonica* 'Variegata', a variegated-leaved variety with smaller red flowers flecked with white.

Slater actively encouraged his ships' captains to collect plant specimens and dispatched botanist-gardeners to scout out likely candidates for his collections, whether by drawing any plants of interest or seizing them. One such individual was John Main, who began his collecting as a very young man – first for George Hibbert and then for Slater in South China, where he was exceedingly vexed by Guangzhou garden design:

> [A] path is made, but so narrow, that it is with much difficulty
> a person can edge himself along it [...] there is even danger of

slipping into the water almost at every step; and this difficulty is called 'pleasure' to the walker himself, or at least to the beholders of his embarrassment! [...] [W]hen leading through a group of trees and shrubs it must pass between the *thickest* of the stems, for no other purpose than to produce annoyance to the pedestrian.

Main appreciates the prominence of gardening and the abundance of plants cultivated by the city's residents, but in his Eurocentricity finds 'nothing interesting' and 'no rational design' in the gardens, deeming them chaotic and 'ridiculous'.

The last voyage he completed for Slater was aboard the *Triton* (an East Indiaman), which arrived back at Gravesend in late September, 1794, having lost its mast in the Channel and damaged the specimens. Nevertheless, the seven rarest plants – camellias and tree peonies – were divided up for their collectors: 'two for His Majesty, two for Sir Joseph Banks, and three for Gilbert Slater, Esq . of Low Layton, Essex', while the other plants – unnamed in the report, so presumably less remarkable – were sent straight to Kew on Joseph Banks' orders. But Slater had died a few months before – too late to enjoy the three specimens of *Paeonia Moutan* or the camellias or indeed the Chinese Elm (*Ulmus parvifolia*) that Main 'introduced' to England. Slater's biography-obituary – written by Main – appears in Britain's first ever horticultural magazine, the snappily-entitled *The Gardener's Magazine and Register of Rural and Domestic Improvement*. It is fulsome indeed in its praise of Slater's persistence – or rather, his finances:

> He spared no expense in pro-curing and cultivating an extensive and well-collected assortment of exotics; and, being all his life connected with East India commerce and shipping, was indefatigable in procuring from them the vegetable beauties described in the writings of Ksempfer, Thunberg, and Du Halde.

He also distributed amongst 'his friends in the China trade' lists of desired plants along with instructions on their collection and transportation – and sent young men like James Main out on his own ships, for 'by unceasing expense, [he] still hoped to possess the beautiful magnolias, the camellias, the paeonies, and azaleas of China'. Unlike James Main, two of the other 'young gardeners' travelling on his ships never returned.

Gilbert Slater is remembered rather more directly in botany via the rose upon which his name is imposed: *R. chinensis semperflorens*, 'Slater's Crimson China', which was thought to have been lost, until 'a mystery rose in Bermuda known there as "Belfield" from the property it grows on was noted by Richard Thomson in 1953'. This rose, a strong scarlet, is thought to actually be 'Slater's Crimson China'. It is telling of the links between slavery, trade and scientific discovery in the British Imperial project that this plant was 'rediscovered' on that island in the North Atlantic Ocean.

I'm standing at the back window in our house, looking over the small gardens that dovetail each other to make this triangular green space between the three terraces. Separate but connected. I'm thinking about the way that each garden, in its layout and features, its plants and stumps and fences, is haunted by the previous occupants and their labour. In ours, there is a yellow scented rose, the main stem lichen-covered, the blooms pale and lushly full. There is a pink camellia, ailing in unsuitable soil, beside it. They link me to plant-collectors and plant-breeders and to the 'other countrysides' of the British colonising project, as well as to the people who lived here before us and who planted and mulched and pruned the space outside our back door.

Other residents have taken on more surprising gardens; at one time there was an entire tropical garden on Lister Road, a few streets away. Apt that a plant fancier should establish such a place, given the road is named after the Lister family, with their botanical interests (slime mould, fungi). The garden gained a write-up in *Country Life* magazine in the nineties and it sounds beautiful. The report itself is extremely entertaining if you are not a regular reader of that journal, not least because after the fifty-six pages of adverts for BMWs and architectural salvage, antique furniture and oil paintings and contemporary sculpture and necklaces made by the Crown Jewellers – and property, so much property, with or without paddocks and often without prices – one is faced with a full-page portrait of a blonde young woman, smiling and neat in neutral makeup, with pearls in her ears and at her throat and the caption beneath announcing that she is about to marry a man.

After all that, the class judgement that thrills through the description of 'Leytonstone, in London's East End, five stops on the Underground from the City' is palpable. The 'East End' as a description is something of a stretch – but it fits with the way in which the report is at pains to emphasise the house as 'outwardly unremarkable, semi-detached and Edwardian' (you can't help but recall those acres and stables and houses with wings and tens of bedrooms that take up the magazine's front pages) and the 'typically worn out, almost inert London "dirt" that had previously passed as soil' – all the more to impress upon the reader the astonishing profusion of hardy, tropical plants the owner has nurtured in his tiny garden – cannas, loquats, bamboo, rice paper and banana plants and tree ferns – inspired, we are told, by Henry Cooke's *A Gloucestershire Garden*, which in turn inspired the 1985 film *The Assam Garden*, directed by Mary McMurray and starring Deborah Kerr.

Cooke was a retired surgeon-general who had been in India during the 1914-18 War; again the 'other countryside' and its people and what the British did there. Across the back gardens from my window, a banana plant waves. In summer, you might see actual bananas – small and green but still recognisable – tucked in tightly against the patterned stems. Palms tower in a couple of other gardens. An orange-gold passionfruit droops from a high wall further down my street, passionflowers adorn a mesh fence at Leyton station. I think of Warner's camellias, of Slater's ships and his crimson rose, lost and found again in Bermuda. They are here because we were there.

Orange Bonnet

Mycena acicula

Like a series of frilly shelves, or like a stack of plates, embedded in the tree. Or that pale, repeating exuberance upon the ornamental plum; our neighbours knock it down each year. It reappears. Or beige stalks, peaked caps, clustered at the foot of the bridleway signpost where it is dark and fissured and coated in growth; sometimes green, sometimes brown, sometimes white. Or the rings that appeared on the playing field, the year the pandemic began, when no one mowed it and there were no training sessions or matches. White buttons surprising a foot that hovers and then mis-steps. And these, two tiny caps, intense orange fading to apricot-cream upon a slender, wavering stalk beside the track, in grass and oak leaf mulching down.

They might be *Mycena acicula*. It has been a wet year and the mushrooms and toadstools and other wet and creeping growths have enjoyed themselves. Orange bonnet mushrooms are common in the UK, but I have never seen them before and their minute brightness seems remarkable to me. They are at home in deciduous woods, where they grow on twigs amongst fallen and rotting leaves and thrive in the damp and deep shade. They were first described by Jacob Christian Schaeffer in 1762, though they went under a different Latin name until 1871. *Acicula* means bristled or needled.

Guilelma Lister was born and died at Sycamore House on Leytonstone High Street. Her father, Arthur, wrote a monograph about mycetozoa – slime moulds – which was published in 1894 and bore illustrations by both himself and Guilelma – Gulie to those who knew her. But Gulie has her own reputation as the 'Queen of Slime Mould', for she went on to study and publish extensively in this field. A large part of her work was done in Leytonstone, though the family had a house in Lyme Regis to which she also repaired.

Lady botanist in her bonnet who studied these strange organisms that are neither one thing nor the other. Like the orange bonnet, a slime mould sports a fruiting body and grows on decaying plant material. But unlike the orange bonnet, it is made of many smaller entities, each a single cell, which can exist quite happily alone but which come together to form structures that will reproduce. The fruiting body. The spores. In Guilelma's day, slime moulds were considered fungi; today they are classed as protozoa – the category of the amoeba. Shape-shifters, taxonomy-smashers. Are they plants? Are they animals? They are neither. They are themselves.

Domestic Shorthair Cat

Felis catus

We used to live with a very old cat. He was nineteen when we inherited him from neighbours who also owned a boxer dog and a tortoise, twenty-six when we took him for his final trip to the vet after twenty-four hours of refusing food and wailing and self-comforting purring. His previous owners swore he was an Outdoors Cat. And indeed, the day they left for Scotland, his 'house' – a kennel with a pointed roof – was lifted over the fence for us to tuck against our back wall. But it didn't take long to realise that Footsie was only an Outdoors Cat because of the dog, and once his canine tormentor had gone (to Scotland, with the tortoise), well. He not only became an Indoors Cat, he became a Back Cat, by which I mean that if you ever found yourself crouched over – sweeping something up, say, reading a broadsheet on the floor, rolling around the carpet with a hot water bottle clamped to your abdomen, say – Footsie could be relied upon to climb onto your back. Laps were fine, backs were better. And outside – pah. *If I must*, his look would say.

'In or out?' We'd stand by the door, he'd stand by the door. We'd all contemplate the outside. There it was: the scrappy grass, the unpruned shrubs, the concrete steps, the broken pots, the kennel, summarily abandoned now he'd got a taste for Inside. Occasionally he'd deign to exit – when Nature called, or when it was sunny. Or when we sprawled on the lawn and he might get the opportunity to sit on a back. But 'in or out' became a catchphrase in our house, and the cat never seemed quite sure.

In a way, he'd found the right humans. Like Footsie, I frequently find myself on the horns of a dilemma, havering on the landing, or in the hallway. In or out? Being privileged, in that I have financial stability, a working partner and employment that allows me to largely work from home, I have that choice. To stay in, though, is sometimes to stagnate in pyjamas, transformed – Tadaah! – into leisure wear by the addition of a pair of socks or a cardigan, to skulk in rooms, pausing doubtfully before a mirror to finger a spot as the washing basket spills its reproaches. Out then. But that's to be surrounded by noise and activity and busy-ness, to subject the self to scrutiny, to field the million tiny needles that come at you from all sides, to risk losing your sense of purpose or separation, to feel the bits of you coming loose and atomising till you can't think.

Finding pockets of quiet in the city – I think of them as feral pockets, for they are often places inhabited by London wildlife – has helped. There is no such thing as silence, as John Cage famously attested, and to pursue such a thing in a city the size of London is surely a wilful, doomed enterprise only embarked upon by the most hardened introvert, but I have found something like it. When the traffic reduces to a background murmur as you hit your stride, half-dreaming down a pavement. Or a blackbird call embellishes your thoughts on a park bench. There is even peace in a Tube carriage, earbuds in, just you and your music, imperfectly heard under the roar and clatter of the train, eyes closed. Of course, an elbow or knee from your fellow passenger might arrive, but for a moment there, you're effectively alone. I'm nowhere near a taxonomy of it, but there are different types of solitude, different kinds of quiet specific to the city.

In the lockdowns following the arrival of SARS-CoV-2, 'out' wasn't possible any more, not in the same way. I couldn't walk by the river any more, or dream on my feet through busy streets, eyes squinting against electric light and traffic fumes at dusk. I couldn't take an off-peak Tube westwards, ride an escalator out of shadow and into daylight like a middle-aged Eurydice. We were all – for months and months on end – very definitely 'in'.

The first lockdown was instructive. I didn't think I'd ever miss the howl and groan of aeroplanes, the holding pattern's frequency, but as I brought in the washing one evening during that first week, the soundscape seemed unnerving in its emptiness. I took my first 'daily walk' on a clear day, the petals sharp and waxy on the narcissi under the corner street tree. Bush Wood and the playing field were busy with walkers. Some solitaries like me turned and went the other way before our paths crossed. Others, in groups of four with dogs, were chatting as if it was any ordinary Saturday. My chest tightened hard at every sighting – *Two metres! Two metres!* – but afterwards I felt reassured. 'Out' wasn't deserted, it was just quieter.

'In', by contrast, was noisier. My beloved was Working From Home. His office door would ricochet off the banisters and out he'd venture, ripping off his wrist supports, fizzing with the latest developments on Chat ('Pets: Cute or Not?'). I could no longer roam free through the house; my imaginary conversations acquired replies. *Did you say something? Are you making tea?*

I made signs. By the end of the second day of working from home together, we each had a YES / NO card to hang from the door knob. Come in / Go Away. I wished I could walk around with a sign round my neck. THINKING.

Of course it cut both ways. I realised I was terrible – really terrible – at respecting my beloved's own boundaries. I wandered in and out of shared spaces and started talking if he was there, with no thought for what I was interrupting – a film, a book, a quiet moment to himself – or if he was working or not. Even his closed office door didn't prevent me from 'popping in' with a quick question or the offer of a cup of tea. But I adjusted. And I began to look forward to the day's punctuations, our tea breaks and shared lunches. Like the punctuation in a sentence, or maybe even like the line and stanza breaks in a poem, they cast new light on the day's proceedings, refocused my endeavours, enabled me to reframe and return to my work.

In the wild, members of the cat family are solitary. So were ancestors of *Felix catus* – but they've adapted. Female feral cats and their kittens will create small social groups near food sources and domestic cats can do this too, if they share their household with another. If they don't bond in this way, then each cat will adopt a separate part of the property as their own – and stay away from the rest.

As I write this now, it's been over ten years since the youngest cat died, and I'm looking at pet adoption websites more frequently. Scrolling through Twitter and Instagram feeds full of the cats of friends and acquaintances, that old longing for an animal companion is strong. The anxieties of the pandemic have brought this into sharper focus. It seems greedy to want more company when I already have a partner – and perhaps a bit foolhardy. My memory of living with cats is of a constant, loving, frustrating battle to keep doors shut and desks and laptops cat-free, of feeling unable to just get up and go to the loo or grab that book from the shelf for fear of disturbing the purring mound on my lap. Of finding it hard to go to sleep or to stretch out my legs for fear of disturbing one of them at the end of the bed, and of being woken by claws hooked into the most unlikely or intimate places when The Royals deem it feeding time. Certainly, I have got more done being pet-free.

Or have I? I think of the time spent staring out of the window, tracking the movements of the neighbours' cats or pausing to stroke a chancer out in the street. I give you, then, an inventory (incomplete) of the neighbourhood's notable residents of the last twenty years:

1. A beaten-up looking ginger tom, possibly stray, named Puke-eater after I watched him lap up a pool of sick one morning. His favourite sport was batting a mouse to another stray beside the fried chicken shop.
2. The epically smelly tabby who ate our cats' food and napped on our furniture and sprayed his piss everywhere and died on a neighbour's sofa. Out of respect for his emphatic ferality, we didn't name him.
3. Fat/Disgusting Cat, who sported a long, luxuriant black-and-white coat until close to the end of its life, when it sported instead a trembling, shaved body and suppurating anus. Owner unknown.
4. Gowron, named after a rather intense Klingon leader from *Star Trek: The Next Generation* on account of her bulging eyes. Actual name: Fifi.
5. His Majesty, the cat who followed Fifi in our neighbours' affections. Likes his food. So do the magpies and foxes, when

his bowl is put outside. He bears this patiently.

6. His Imperial Naughtiness, who likes people, other cats, foxes, exploring other houses, and His Majesty's dinners.

7. The tortoiseshell at the corner who sits in wait for commuters in the evening, will call to you across a junction.

8. The white-and-black who lives near the tortoiseshell. Maybe lives with the tortoiseshell. May be, in fact, two white-and-black cats. Hides under cars.

9. And our two, who died eventually as old cats do of organ failure at nineteen and twenty-six respectively. Susie and Footsie, names inadequate to their true natures.

Hawthorn

Crataegus monogyna

It is the day after the Vernal Equinox. I've had a difficult winter, a Slug Winter, in which I mostly lay in bed and scrolled through the news. But the days are about to lengthen and I am going for walks again, exploring a range of routes that take me onto the section of Wanstead Flats between Lake House and Centre Roads. It's a roughly triangular area bordered by traffic, with its apex just below a roundabout and a large pond at its foot. In the centre, there's a small patch of woodland containing a double row of trees that looks like part of an avenue, and a number of silver birch and oaks spreading out from it. The northern part of this triangle – the part I have taken to stomping and scowling around – has been designated a Site of Special Scientific Interest, due to the importance of the acid grassland that characterises it, although these terrains also continue eastwards across the road. In this patch of land, heather can be found – rare elsewhere in Epping Forest – as well as other plants characteristic of heathland: tormentil, sheep's sorrel, heath bedstraw, mat-grass, heath grass, heath rush, sheep's-fescue. My plant-identifying eyes aren't sufficiently focused to see them amid the ever-present broom, but I do recognise the clumps of heather. This land is good for insects – particularly solitary bees and wasps – and migratory birds. There are skylarks and meadow pipits, birds whose declining UK populations are cause for great concern. Natural England, assessing the area in 2010, noted the problems with air quality – all that traffic causes nitrogen pollution of the soil, changing its pH, affecting which plants can grow – but for now, it's here; a remarkable habitat in an East London postcode.

It's a strange landscape to my eyes, which travel unimpeded over its low contours to the bordering roads with their heavy traffic. It is populated by crows that call from treetops or watch me with an unnerving directness as they stalk or hop out of my path. When I first start walking here, the plants and grasses look stunted; many of the trees seem scorched and the abundant broom (*Cytisus scoparius*) is barely knee-high. There was a terrible fire in 2018 that filled the air with smoke visible all over the city.

Reputedly the 'largest ever grassfire' in London, it needed forty fire engines to vanquish it, and firefighters had to remain onsite for two days to damp down the land and prevent the flames from reigniting. The Flats barely had time to recover before more fires broke out in 2020. The ground is parched in these Anthropocene summers; grassfires only need one dropped cigarette, strong sun through broken glass.

Now though, the land is wet – there has been much rain – and there are a lot of puddles of varying sizes. I watch the crows fluster and shimmy as they bathe, picking my way between clumps of broom. One positive effect of the fire was to keep this stuff in check; it was planted in the late 1880s, when the land passed into the hands of the City of London Corporation, following the Epping Forest and Open Spaces Acts, sparked by a mass protest at the enclosure of some parts of Wanstead Park by its then owner. The Flats – so-called because of the sandy gravel beneath (deposited thousands of years ago by the Thames) – were sown with grass after drainage, made – well, *flatter* – and planted with saplings. Two hundred years before these 'improvement' works, the land was much wetter, the trees were sparser – and sheep and cattle grazed freely. Although there are 'Beware Cattle' signs further north near Hollow Ponds, I've not seen a cow around here. The boundaries of three London Boroughs meet upon this land, but it's designated as part of Epping Forest.

Something catches my eye, a flutter on one of the bare, scrubby trees ahead. Litter, I think. 'Witches' knickers', I've heard them called; carrier bags and helium balloons caught in branches. But these are ribbons, tied into bows. An orange one, a satiny purple one, a gauzy white one, one that looks like a black lace garter. I count them; there are six in total. They are tied to the ends of branches roughly the same height, at regular intervals around the tree, describing a circle. Witches indeed; I've heard of rituals around this time of year, the repurposing of Easter by NeoPagans into Ostara or Eostre. Could Leytonstone have its very own coven? But I think also of the custom of tying your wish in cloth form to the branch of a tree that is special in some way, maybe because it's in a place associated with the supernatural. A Wishing Tree.

I make a special point of visiting the tree again on May the First – Beltane – hoping to catch a possible coven in the act, or evidence at least that they've returned. But the only people out and about are some dogwalkers and the odd jogger. A couple of young men have strung a belt or something on an oak bough and are practicing chin-ups.

The ribbons and garter are still there, tied – I see now, as leaves have appeared – to burnt ends jutting out from the tree's living green core like arms or the spokes of a wheel. Maybe they wanted to heal the tree? Protect the land from fires? The leaves are small and lobed and clusters of tiny white flowers seem about to break into bloom. It's hawthorn; a significant plant in British folklore, said to be unlucky if you bring it into the house, and not a tree to loiter beside, since it's reputed to be the habitual meeting place for fairies.

The next time I visit, the flowers are in bloom. In fact, all the hawthorns are in bloom and I'm assailed by that familiar, giddy smell I always associate with early summer. It is described as being like almonds with an edge of sex. Hawthorns forming part of an avenue between Bush Wood and Fred Wigg tower. Hawthorns bordering the track by the playing field. Hawthorns upon the heath.

Skylark

Alauda arvensis

A rippling. Does it burble? Does it call throatily?
From so high, skylark, last heard on a Yorkshire moor.

Here on the heath, it is early spring. Amongst the broom, there are tufts of tough grass and coins of earth and moss scattered about by crows, jackdaws and magpies, searching for goodness, tasty grubs and beetles, all the crawling things. The birds nest in the oaks on Wanstead Flats – more Victorian planting like the broom – and in spring the grass beneath is often scattered with twigs they have dropped.

I step over the corvids' litter. I am having trouble with sleep and walk as much as I can in my free time to tire myself out. Catkins have appeared on the willows; some acidic yellow in amongst the rough grass and broom, some a fuzzy white nearer the path. A small flock of long-tailed tits has been keeping pace with me. The paths and tracks are boggy again, with all the recent rain.

As I cross the road between the pollarded ash tree and the mobile phone mast, I'm drawn to a length of green plastic fencing. Since I've been last, a whole section of the Flats adjacent to Aldersbrook has been fenced off. This part of the heath has a lot of heather in its wilder parts, but it's also where people fly their model aircraft. At the eastern edge, a carpark is busy with people and geese, swans, ducks give loud voice on Alexandra Lake.

Fencing off the Flats is not new. There was the work Thames Water did to install piping for the Beckton Desalination Plant, digging up the playing field and festooning it with orange netting. There was the year that Waltham Forest became the first ever London Borough of Culture, and a scrappy part of grass between the Green Man roundabout and Bush Road was transformed into a music venue for an *Africa Express* gig. By the time we'd heard about it, the tickets had all sold out. Roads were closed, the event happened and eventually the concrete blocks and crash barriers were removed and we could access the paths and the land again; newly sporting large squares of bare earth and mud in amongst the grass and wildflowers.

I am gloomy as I approach the plastic fencing. Another event? More infrastructure works? The fires have already wreaked their trouble. What now?

When I first moved here, a smoulder hung perpetually in the air around Bush Wood. One of the keepers came across me one morning, standing undecided beside a dome of holly which had smoke puttering out from its base.

'Been like that for months.' He shrugged inside his green bodywarmer. 'Burn itself out, eventually.'

In those days, as the very late nineties slid into the early 2000s, the scent of woodfire hung around the high-grown thickets all summer, and it was hard to believe the prediction that our climate would get wetter as it got hotter. Of course, we know better now. Nearby Walthamstow flooded last year and temperatures in the late 30s Celsius are a regular local summer feature. These days, the keepers mow wide areas around the paths, creating firebreaks and leaving a swathe of grasses and wildflowers nearer the trees.

And they are taking other action to conserve the Flats;

action that is bearing fruit. The Superintendent's report for a particular summer noted hopeful signs: a pair of skylarks feeding their chicks, five males singing – an increase from the previous year. Nests on the ground are vulnerable to dogs and feet and fire – so this year, there are the green plastic fences around heather and grass, and the carpark is closed during breeding season.

I read the laminated sign stapled to a fence post and walk along the boundary. It's an unfamiliar feeling, this hopefulness. You won't believe me, I know – I scarcely believed it myself – but as I walked the green length of plastic, I swear I heard it, that bubbling ripple of sound, high up.

Ash

Fraxinus excelsior

Early to bed and the last light of the evening is reflected in the windows opposite. A bathroom light goes on. The terrace of houses across the gardens from ours turns like an ocean liner into the dusk. The catch on my window rattles in the wind, the curtains open to the strange twilight that exists in summer between half-nine and forever, when the underside of clouds are orange-tinged and cloudless skies are bluebell. In this night, the tree seen over the rooftops is forming shapes in the near-dark as the wind tosses it about. Its boughs seem to be full of people, a communal dipping and bowing and rocking side-to-side. On the right, lovers seem to couple, then it is an orgy, the fucking happening in a chain of pushing and sliding and separating and thrusting. Then the wind dissolves it and brings out instead a parent and child; the larger mass of leaves seeming to hold the small body up to the air for joy, then bringing it down to its chest.

Plant names hold within themselves the key to their nature. If you didn't have access to any other information, you could still learn a lot just by knowing a plant's botanical name. My tree is *Fraxinus excelsior*, the European ash. *Fraxinus*, from the Latin for spear, ash wood being used historically to make the shafts of spears. You might describe the shape of the ash tree's leaves as spear-like: long and curved slightly to a point, set opposite each other on the stem. *Excelsior*, meaning ever upwards, even higher.

And its common name, too, from *æsc*, a word that has also travelled (though from colder places than Rome), that also holds the shafts of spears, as the ash tree does, in its trunk, its branches. Yggdrasil, the Norse world tree, is an ash. The first man, Askr, is named Ash. Man and spear. Or man and guitar? Bruce Springsteen's Telecaster on the cover of *Born to Run* has a body made of (swamp) ash.

Ash is a hardwood, used where resilience is needed, and strength. *Fraxinus excelsior*, rising from tarmac, the trunk powering upwards like a spear or a sword held high. I draw aside the curtain – and in the light reflected back to the city from the cloud (it is never dark here), I see the lovers and parents and children swaying slightly in silhouette above the solid prow of the terraced houses.

I visit my ash the next morning. It is a marvel. Verdant. Huge. It rises from a small square of earth bounded by concrete aggregate and edging stones. Ash tree, *Fraxinus excelsior*, rising from pavement beside road, rising above grey hard surfaces. Its leaves appear along a branch in bunches, clumps and don't quite resemble the pictures I find online. Those clumps make it look more like narrow-leaved ash, *Fraxinus angustifolia*.

Ash burns with a fierce heat. The druid wand is of ash. Venus of the Woods; the seeds are for divination, for power over the water. Ash heals small children, if you pass them through a cleft in the trunk and bind it afterwards. Naturalist Gilbert White, writing from Selborne in the eighteenth century, observes such trees:

> [i]n a farmyard near the middle of this village stands, at this day, a row of pollard-ashes, which, by the seams and long cicatrices down their sides, manifestly show that, in former times, they have been cleft asunder.

The trees' two halves, he writes, would have been wedged apart, in order to perform the ceremony: children of the village would be 'stripped naked [and] pushed through the apertures', after which action, each tree was 'plastered with loam, and carefully swathed up.' If the tree healed, then the child would be cured, but if the tree did not, and the cleft remained, then the 'operation' was assumed not to have worked. 'Having occasion to enlarge my garden not long since, I cut down two or three such trees', White goes on. He does not, it can be supposed, subscribe to any such beliefs in the power of the cleft ash.

Even stranger is another tree that stood near the village church until the vicar had it felled and burnt. It was 'a very old grotesque hollow pollard ash, which for ages had been looked on with no small veneration as a shrew-ash.' This, White explains, is a tree from which twigs or branches can be taken, in order to stroke 'the limbs of cattle' which have been in contact with a shrew:

> for it is supposed that a shrew-mouse is of so baneful and deleterious a nature, that wherever it creeps over a beast, be it horse, cow, or sheep, the suffering animal is afflicted with cruel anguish, and threatened with the loss of the use of the limb.

To guard against this terrible affliction, the village always ensured it kept a shrew-ash – which, 'once medicated, would maintain its virtue for ever.' As for how such a tree is created, White leaves his reader in no doubt. It's every bit as cruel as you might imagine:

> [I]n the body of the tree a deep hole was bored with an auger, and a poor devoted shrew-mouse was thrust in alive, and plugged in, no doubt, with several quaint incantations long since forgotten.

Since the ceremonial words have been forgotten, he assures his reader, the practice has not survived, and there are no shrew-ashes left in use in the region.

Later that year, I realise why the tree looks different to the ones in the books. I open the curtains in the back room one morning to be confronted with the sight of a man, suspended from a branch above the rooftops, chainsaw swinging from a toolbelt. I watch as he steadies himself, checks his harness, adjusts his ear defenders. The sound of chainsaws grinds through the neighbourhood – and the next time I look over the gardens, neither man nor branches are visible. The council has been out pollarding.

Street trees, with their roots so thirsty for the scant supplies of water they receive, so cramped by pipes and compacted earth, have a cruelly short life. The London planes that storm Bloomsbury with their fluff in late summer, the lime trees dripping honeydew onto parked cars below, this ash shooting ever upward; they will ail and die much sooner than in the 'wild'. And they'll be replaced with smaller trees, less ambitious for space. Cherries spring into blossom along one street, I pass a gingko biloba along another.

It's always struck me as an extraordinary act of faith, to plant a tree like ash. Whoever decided that our road needed trees knew they would never see them in maturity. Who was he? A property developer? A municipal works officer? Regardless, he was one of many across North and East London, laying out the terrain for the new suburbs springing up in the wake of the Cheap Trains Act of 1864. Rows and rows of terraced housing were constructed in places like Tottenham, West Ham, Walthamstow and what was then called Leyton, in anticipation of the so-called respectable working-class who would take full advantage of the new 'workmen's fare' and the convenience of a short commute by train to work: securely-employed men who would make reliable tenants if they couldn't purchase the houses, 'skilled artisans, policemen and firemen, railway engineers or gaffers in the gasworks'.

Here in Leytonstone, our parade was built in the first decade of the twentieth century – like the row facing us across our gardens, over which the ash looms. You can see the swift spread of this 'railway suburb' very clearly on the old maps: the Ordnance Survey of 1863 shows only fields, in place of our network of streets, and isolated structures – such as the mysterious Swiss Cottage, which was pulled down some time in the mid-twentieth-century. What I know as The Avenue – a double row of limes that peters out into wild rose bushes, topped by a small woodland and fringed by the playing field – is marked clearly, linked to a triangular arrangement of rows at its head.

When the map is revised in 1893-4, things have changed radically. The Swiss Cottage, Lake House (where the poet Thomas Hood – and his son Tom, also a writer – lived for a time) are still there, but the fields are gone. Our network of streets are clearly laid out and named, lightly peppered with houses in pairs or small rows of four or less. The 1891 Census records two households on Woodville Road: a widow and her domestic help in one house, and a civil servant and his wife next door with their eight children – the eldest boys are clerks. The parade containing our house is absent, but it's my guess that the trees that make our neighbourhood so pleasant – or their predecessors – were planted around then.

I discover all this during lockdown. Unable to visit the local archives, I have taken to the web and find myself on family history sites, determinedly tracking the growth of houses on our street and following the residents of Woodville Road and their movements far beyond the late nineteenth century.

Ten years after the widow and civil servant, more houses have been built on the street; the residents' occupations include that of county council clerk, schoolmistress, boarding housekeeper, dressmaker, butcher shop keeper, music hall artist, publishing clerk, commercial traveller, jobbing gardener and journalists – these last a woman and her adult son. By 1911, all forty-four addresses on our street are present, including our own. Our house, spanking new with its moulded plaster and large bay windows, is occupied by a family of five. The father works as a dock warehouse keeper – a promotion from his former job as clerk. He hasn't moved far; he was born in Stratford, just down the High Road, the eldest of four sons – and lived with his wife and newborn daughter in Forest Gate before moving to Leytonstone. A year after the census, the family have moved and the youngest, a daughter, is born in Romford. There's no record for the house in 1921's Census – where had they gone? – and it's recorded as standing empty in 1939, when everyone in Great Britain had to register their details in preparation for war.

Why do I hunt so far into the night for this information? Sheer nosiness, perhaps – but I realise that it's also because this is home. Cut a hazel twig and shove it into the soil and eventually, if it's had enough water and the soil is good, it will grow roots. I belong to the house and I belong to Leytonstone and I'm interested in the other people who also called it home. I share its history with them, now. I am a local.

This still surprises me. My childhood was somewhat peripatetic, moving not just between houses but counties, cities, countries. I've never really been able to say I was from anywhere and I envied the kids at my schools who'd always lived in the same house. They'd talk casually about going round their gran's for tea or playing with their cousins at the weekend and I'd have nothing to offer in return. I didn't seem to have any roots at all apart from some far-off connection to Wales, maybe. When we settled in the Forest of Dean, I didn't really believe that we would stay – though my family did and it was I who moved away.

I didn't really feel that I belonged in London either, but then nor did anybody else, it seemed. There were so many of us who were from elsewhere and this comforted me, for London could make room for us all. And anyway, when I first moved to the city, I didn't want to belong anywhere. I didn't want to be identifiable. I loved just being a person, sitting on a bus or walking down a pavement, going into a shop, just one of the anonymous millions going about their business. I was no one and so, subject to no scrutiny, interesting to no one, I could get on with my life.

But that has changed. Now we are among the long-term residents of the area and I've learnt the pleasure of knowing my neighbours' names, of swapping things for the garden and chatting. The local kids have grown up and new families moved in, with a different menagerie of pets. One of the lime trees on our street loses a limb in a storm – taking out someone's wing mirror and a power line in the process – and the Council come to chop it up and clear the pavement. The road's resurfaced, the parking rules change (several times), the sodium streetlights are replaced with low energy bulbs and the old folks' home opposite is converted into flats. I love the sense of it all going on around me, of being part of these seemingly ordinary things that make up our shared, local history. That old longing from my years as a 'new kid' has found its answer. Where am I from? Here. Life is rich if you stay put for long enough.

The tree surgeon in his harness wields the chainsaw with confidence and more branches topple from the ash. Soon the name is an aspiration rather than a description; blunt stubby tips, then even these disappear from view as the tree's height is reduced. Name as marker of change. Name as memorial.

Or name as statement of intent. Name as hope. *Fraxinus excelsior.* Onward and upward, I tell myself.

As the year turns its wheel, I miss the sight of those fronds over the rooftops. I become anxious about the street trees' health. Our lime – the one I lie in bed and stare at from the main bedroom – has lichen and moss growing on it – and in the fierce heat of July, the leaves drop early and in large quantities. Ash dieback disease (Chalara), confirmed in the UK in 2012 but thought to have appeared as early as 2002, is caused by a fungus named *Hymenoscyphus fraxineus* and has infected trees up and down the UK. Might it kill mine? I do a little digging around online and am reassured; the fungus finds it harder to travel in urban landscapes. Tiny white mushrooms appear on infected leaf litter; they get a better chance to spread their spores in woodland, where this won't be cleared away by streetsweepers and the temperature and atmosphere's more hospitable and humid than a London pavement. If a tree is under stress already – lack of water and scorching are two main problems faced by urban trees

– then it may succumb to an infection, but this won't necessarily be Chalara. So it seems my ash is safe for now.

The following summer, I look over at the rooftops one evening: *Fraxinus excelsior*, uppermost shoots as tall as the chimneys. Ever upward.

White-cheeked Turaco

Tauraco leucotis

A bird about the size of a wood pigeon. The first time I see it, I am walking past a garden shrub full of berries and disturb the birds feeding there. Wood pigeons, I think, from the clattery fluster of their wings, as they perch in a nearby London Plane. But one of them chirrups in an extremely not-wood-pigeony way, and when I look up, its silhouette and colour are somewhat different. It is dark, I think, and a little smaller. The neck is doing something strange, the head is decidedly not wood-pigeony, and what is that red around its face? The internet yields a black woodpecker, but the beak is wrong, and it sits in the tree very differently.

A few days later, I see the bird again, on the apex of the roofs opposite. Definitely a dark back, definitely not a wood pigeon or woodpecker. I take to the Internet.

It is famous. The White-Cheeked Turaco of Leytonstone. Apart from the white cheeks that provide its common name, it has a circle of red around its eyes, a red beak and a ruff that sticks up like the plume on an eighteenth-century military hat. These and the kink in its neck makes it look a bit gormless and foolish, to me. A clown bird. Improbable. Yet here it is.

Tauraco leucotis is usually found in Eritrea, Ethiopia and South Sudan, particularly where there is forest – for example high in the Ethiopian Highlands, where it feeds on plants and berries such as juniper and podocarpus. It is not a migratory bird. The internet seems to be full of information for would-be breeders and owners of turacos; the white-cheeked is considered the 'easiest' to keep and care for. Captive birds were first bred in the UK in 1964, according to the International Turaco Society, so ours, like the bird seen in Cardiff last year, or the ringed one seen in Havant over 2019 and 2020, is an escapee.

I'm taking my daily walk, nearly a decade after my first sighting of the turaco and pass the cotoneaster where I saw it. Is it still around? Alive? How long do these birds live? I am still thinking about it as I pass the whitebeam saplings in the clearing near the Quakers' wall. As if on cue, a chirrup emits from a nearby oak. Is it the turaco? As I'm staring up into foliage, a guy walks past with his dog – a fluffy Arctic-looking one, curled-over tail, blue eyes, pale fawn and grey and white – and stops as he notices me shading my eyes and trying to pick the squawkers out from the branches of the oaks. We start chatting, and he remarks on all the different birds there are in Bush Wood.

'Even an African mountain bird', he says. 'It only comes out when it's cold and foggy.'

He must mean the white-cheeked turaco. Bird of mystery, resolved solid by condensation.

'And lots of different parrots!' His dog settles down on the grass. No, he doesn't mean the parakeets – they're locals now. But escaped pets, like the turaco, taken to the trees, to the Forest and a wilder life, infinite variety above the heads of the mountain bikers, the couples having their quickies, the dogwalkers. He tells me about the man whose lizard escaped while he was cleaning the cage: 'Ended up here. Three-foot lizard!' This was maybe four years ago. 'It's probably dead now.'

We enthuse together a bit more about the wood and the creatures it harbours until his dog springs to its feet and starts whining. It's caught wind of something – another dog? A cat? A deer? – and we say our goodbyes. He walks off, dog straining at the end of the lead.

The turaco, the lizard. The wood. The heath. Here be dragons. Here be the myths. A place for Borges's Imaginary Beings. Bush Wood and the Flats as a receptacle for escaped wildlife – flora, fauna, avia. Hops, honesty, bluebells, the parakeets. Apparently now there's also a blue budgie after someone's pet escaped. Land of mythical beasts, an alt-Borough in an alt-London. I don't expect to see the bird again – it's been over ten years – but it still exists, here on the muddy tracks, above the bramble and fern, the discarded dogshit bags and cans of lager. Between the graffitied trees. Like Schrödinger's famous cat, these creatures are all potential. Potentially real, potentially not, in this place that is not quite Narnia, or Arcadia, or the Forest of Arden, but nonetheless an in-between space, bordered by roads and suburban housing, edging the city and the fields. The wood and the heath are places people come to find the beautiful, to be with Nature and to find their other selves, the ones who run or walk or cycle, who wear different clothes – gym kit, wellies – who maybe think a bit differently for a while. A way of being is conjured up – beings are conjured up – which might quite easily bleed into the everyday.

Connected to that is the way in which the wood and the

heath offer the *otium* of the Pastoral; that pleasant suspension of one's everyday activities (i.e. work). When I am out in the green places on my doorstep, I'm offered a suspended moment of idyll that interrupts the daily and the everyday and inserts into it notions of another time, another place, one that only exists in my imagination. It might be only a possibility or promise, fleeting rather than permanent, but it is powerful. It is the feral borough.

A few days later, someone posts a picture on social media – a black blotch, mid-air as if hurdling a chimney pot – taken in Wanstead. It is the white-cheeked turaco. The same one? A different one? Are they multiplying?

Hops

Humulus lupulus

No, it's hops, I'm sure of it. I take a photo on my phone because my beloved is sceptical.

Later, when I look at it, finger grease has blurred the lens so that each cone is surrounded by a halo. Hops, you seem to glow by your own light, draped like a skein of Christmas bulbs over a field maple, roadside, where the grass grows longer towards the bushes at the Quakers' boundary wall. Where did you come from?

For years, East London provided the Kent hopfields with pickers in late summer; a family holiday, earning a bit of money, out in the fresh air. Then, as mechanisation was introduced in the 1950s, the hop-picking holiday declined. But hops, it seems, have returned.

My hops, glowing near the Green Man roundabout connecting us with Essex, the M11, the M25 and beyond may be an escapee – borne in birdshit? In the sole of a shoe? – from one of the hop-growing initiatives set up by the new, small breweries that have been established in this area.

Such an initiative is the Walthamstow Beer Hop project, run by the not-for-profit East London Brewing Company, where local residents are encouraged to grow their own hop plants and harvest the cones for the Company's use in September, after which they're invited to spend a day at the Brewery to learn about beer production. The culmination is the launch event, where the hop-growers get to taste the green-hopped ale their plants have helped produce. Participants buy their hop plants and pay a sign-up fee – this is hop-growing and -picking as pleasant and nostalgic hobby, rather than paid, outdoors work.

Hops have other uses than flavouring beer. You can cook the shoots the way you would asparagus. The resin contains a phytoestrogen – a hormone similar to the one involved in breastfeeding – and it used to be thought that hops could help encourage milk production. Later studies have suggested that the opposite is the case. The plant remains in use, though, as a sedative. Look at the ingredients of any herbal sleeping tablets and it's likely that along with valerian, they contain hops.

Revenant cones and bines, scratched hands dream-remember you. Tangled by the road, you conjure hop yards.

Nos

Vapor risus

A clutch of sleek miniature bottles in the gutter by a grating. A single, flattened one, kicked across the pavement. And in the woods I see uninflated balloons, yellow and blue. Aw, I think, someone having a party. Kids' voices somewhere in the wood, little kids and a parent. Birthday party, I think, remembering the images on social media of friends celebrating outside. It is still cold but it is safer outside, with the infection rates as they are, and no vaccine yet. Aerosols, breath particles dispersed.

But then, those silver canisters beside the balloons. Not that kind of party, then.

For years I thought the stuff was called *Nox*, like the Latin for night. Nox, the Roman version of Nyx, Greek Goddess of Night – 'who dictates to gods and men alike', who even Zeus himself will not cross – wears a crown of darkness, a crown of mist, comes swiftly when called. She is mother of the Fates, of Sleep, Pain, Strife and Death.

Nos, Noz, Balloons, Whippits, Laughing Gas, Chargers, Hippie Crack. When inhaled, usually from a balloon, nitrous oxide can bring euphoria, a state of calm, the giggles, dizziness, hallucinations, nausea. It smells of nothing, contains no colour, slows the mind. When measured and mixed with oxygen, it's pain relief in childbirth. With balloons, in the deep of woods, it is illegal. So many sharpnesses and accidents into, onto which to fall, in the dark and deep night. Nox, Nos, filling the lungs; too full of it, the brain is starved and damaged, the body comes to harm.

In 2010, Anne Carson's extraordinary work of memorial, *Nox*, was published by New Directions. It is a box, inside which is a long concertina of folded card, on which, amongst other things, the poet presents us with multiple attempts upon a translation of a poem by Catullus; number 101, one of three elegies he wrote for his brother. There are definitions of and ruminations upon key words that appear in the poem, photographs, scraps of letters and notes, as well as Carson's own narrative. The reverse of the box bears a statement, in capital letters, as if an inscription on a monument. Which it is, of a sort:

WHEN MY BROTHER DIED I MADE AN EPITAPH FOR
HIM IN THE FORM OF A BOOK. THIS IS A REPLICA
OF IT, AS CLOSE AS WE COULD GET.

It is a beautiful thing, this epitaph. A solid block that then unfolds, opening into a chain of pieces, a spiral meditation. It haunts or is haunted by. It mimics so closely the repetitive nature of mourning; the returning to and parsing out of fragments, evidence, memory. The attempts upon understanding. The reaching-out-to the lost one.

'Nox, frater, nox'. The night, my brother, and the night.

The hiding face of night, her softening mists. One letter away from *nox* is *noxa*, harm, from which derives the word *noxious*.

    Nox, Goddess of Night, keep safe the woman with the jacket over her head, inhaling deeply near the bins behind the block of flats. Keep safe the ones with blue and yellow balloons. Grant them only sleep. The numbers keep on rising, each one of them a person missed, here in the ordinary, daylight world. You have enough.

> *Good night, ladies. Good night, sweet ladies. Good night, good night.*

Common Wood Pigeon

Columba palumbus

I am walking from the rural train station towards the flat my parents 'downsized' to a few years ago. I've had a call; Dad's time is limited, more limited than any of us thought. The cancer has evaded the drugs and radiotherapy that tamped it down for ten years and seeded in his liver, and his health is declining fast. I cross the road from the car park, I take the footbridge over the stream and pass the industrial park on the town's outskirts. It is unseasonably hot this year and everything is flowering early. Between the pavement and the high metal fence are banks of hedgerow flowers: dog rose, bramble, something else I can't name with soft cloches of yellow blooms.*

---

* It turns out to be large-flowered evening primrose (*Oenothera glazioviana*); introduced as a garden

When I get to the flat, I am extremely sweaty. The door and windows are open and an electric fan is keeping the temperature bearable. My dad is thin and dapper in a checked seersucker shirt. He looks tired.

Later I go with my mother to a garden centre, to buy a garden umbrella. 'Get him outside for a bit,' she says. 'Fresh air: he's cooped up all day.'

We assemble the contraption with much hooting on my part: Dad insists on coming outside to supervise, even though standing up for more than a couple of minutes exhausts him. He ends up reclining on the grass of the communal gardens while I try to match up bolt and hole, nut and riser. There is a slight breeze and a little shade. It feels good to be outside, slipping into my familiar, bumbling, left-handed awkwardness around objects, chiding my dad for insisting on standing, on trying to organise and instruct, when he should be relaxing, resting, conserving his strength. (Not hastening his dying, I want to say to him. I have a Big Job Interview coming and can't stay long this time. I'm aware I've been appraising him since I got here: how thin? How ill? How long has he got? He sleeps a lot, but can walk about, is still eating – not a lot, a kiddies' portion to our platefuls, but still, it's eating.)

---

plant, originally in the 1600s, now growing ferally, dispersed along railway lines, multiplying its hybrids so that identification can be tricky.

We sit out under the new umbrella and eat our tea. I have disentangled some fold-out chairs and a table from the ladder in the shed and we balance our meal on the table's wobble. The sky is intense, the town is quiet, the shadows lengthen. A willow susurrates in the light wind and we watch the swifts screaming past.

'This is perfect,' my dad says, tracking their veering zig-zags. 'Isn't this lovely?'

A wood pigeon assents.

He dies very early on the morning of my Big Interview. I am in a hotel room in Norwich, ironing a dress.

'He'd want you to go through with it,' my sister says. She's just returned from the hospital, the fatigue cracking her voice.

In between presentation and interview, I slip off alone to sit on a concrete bench on a concrete walkway. Everything is altered, every sense impression falls upon me with an intensity that seems to slow down time and render each second monolithic and important. It is hot here too; I catch the resinous smell of the conifer opposite the walkway. Its boughs creak. I study my feet, trying to decide whether to jack it all in or not. I could go to the kind receptionist who gave me a badge and stowed my case away beside her knees and tell her I'm dropping out. So far things haven't been too bad, I tell myself, although I'm aware I'm interacting with the staff and other candidates a little more intensely than I would normally. (They are all lovely. I am convinced we will all stay in touch afterwards. I want to give them all the job.) But a familiar sliding feeling has started up inside me. I shouldn't be here. I am the weakest of all the candidates. My performance is beyond disappointing and I can read it on the panellists' faces. This is a rare chance and I am screwing it up because I do not really deserve it. I am shit and the interviewers know it.

I cringe as I think of the questions that followed my presentation. They seemed to be in an alien language or using concepts I had never encountered, and I kept having to ask for clarification. I looked at one of the interviewers – a former colleague I knew from my PhD days – and marvelled at the gulf that opened up between his question and any plausible answer I might give. It is a very usual, very normal question to ask an interviewee, but I could not for the life of me think of what to say.

The only time I think I am going to start crying is when I and a couple of other interviewees arrive late to the Candidates' Lunch. The sight of finger food and bottles of sparkling water spread out on trestle tables in a deserted hall, the prospect of negotiating the selection of appropriate food and having to eat and chat freezes me on the threshold. I hear my voice wobble as I make my excuses and rush out before the wobble becomes anything more.

Now I am sitting on this bench, looking at my feet and a pine cone that has fallen next to them. It feels like an offering, consolation, meant just for me. The glare of pale concrete, the sun on my back. A wood pigeon calling. I think about picking up the cone – but then I would have to walk into the interview with it in my hand. Where would I put it?

Sweetness: high, piercing, chatty. A goldfinch in the pine's crown. I remember these birds from when I lived in this city; I hadn't really encountered them before then and was enchanted by the yellow cheeks, the jaunty red and black stripes. The song, all bubbling liquid and chatter, unspools, blithe, above.

A pied wagtail lands a few feet away from me, runs, halts, runs. Its mate is calling from a nearby building.

I don't fall apart, but I don't acquit myself well either. The faces of the interviewers seem to manifest the voices in my head that grow fiercer as the day wears on and the temperature climbs. *You're shit. You're blagging. You're a bullshitter. Two TWO two two.* The wood pigeon from my undergraduate days is haunting me.

The day of my finals was hot like today and I and my friends had been drinking since the morning when the sheets of paper went up outside Senate House. The sliding feeling inside my torso as my eyes slid further and further down the pinned-up pages is the same feeling I have now. Fear and hope tugging against the undertow, then succumbing to that deep sucking current which isn't disappointment, isn't even dismay. It is the knowledge that I was right all along; I am an interloper and a fool. I am stupid and uncivilized. This secret knowledge that kept me perpetually embarrassed as an undergraduate – too embarrassed to ask the questions that might help me in my studies – has surfaced with the wood pigeon's call. *Two TWO, two two. Two TWO, two two.*

The journey home is a long one; signalling problems or trespassers on the lines or lack of train crew or train taken out of service mean I have to take a diversion, and I leave my case on a train as I hurry to make a connection. I arrive home much later than planned, thirsty, barely making any sense, and spend the next hour trying to track down my luggage.

I don't get the job. *You failed you failed you failed you ran away and chased a job you didn't get you didn't see him as he died you didn't tell him you loved him you failed you failed you failed you failed you failed you failed you failed you FOOL you you fool, you FOOL you you fool, you FOOL you you fool, you*

Common Kestrel

Falco tinnunculus

Storm Evert has just blown through and I take a midday walk in sunshine to see the wrack of broken branches, the litter clogging drain grates, the bins on their sides. Walking in Bush Wood is like walking on a soap bar left too long in its dish – except the surface is even more gelid and shifting than that – and there are deep mud patches churned up by feet and bike tyres, puddles everywhere. Parakeets start up their shrieking as I walk around the pond-become-marsh-become-now-almost-a-lake; the waterline is nearly up to the basin it sits in. I haven't ever seen it this full. In recent years, rushes, then grasses and willows have colonised the pond and it looks like it's in the process of changing from a marsh into something more solid. Today, though, I have to edge past bramble on a narrow, muddy strip of land in order to avoid the water.

A kestrel and crow are above me on a dead tree – casualty of one of the fires in the very dry years of the early 2000s which dried up the water, leaving a stink and a surface of cracked, peanut butter-coloured mud. They share the same branch, the crow testing twigs for its nest, edging nearer as it tugs with its beak. Small birds – blue tits – mount raids on bushes around and below the bigger birds. They seem remarkably bold, given that kestrels eat blue tits.

The crow feints and karks at the kestrel, which flinches.* It is smaller than the crow, with a greyish head and a red-brown back. A male, then. Females are larger, have far less grey. Is it ill?

My dad loved birds of prey. His most-prized sighting was a golden eagle, up in Scotland. He and my mother had booked themselves on a bird-watching holiday, the sort where you're guided by professionals and all stay in the same hotel. The last time I saw

---

* The crow is more properly called the carrion crow, *Corvus corone*. We have many around the Flats; vocal and bold. They don't eat blue tits, though they will take the eggs. I once saw a crow make off from our garden with a very small, dead fox cub, which couldn't have been more than a few days old. It hung inert from the crow's talons as the bird laboured in flight. A single eyeball and a bloody patch, slightly sticky, were all that remained.

him before he died, he talked excitedly about it, about how I should go too, that I loved nature so I'd enjoy it, and he bundled up the paperwork left over from that spring trip and shoved it into my hands.

There, he said. *My legacy.*

As I waited for the small, local train to pull out of the station the next day, I stared hard out of the window, fiddling with the envelope, trying to stuff it further into my overpacked rucksack. I willed Dad to hang on till I could visit again at the weekend, pushing away what my eyes and ears had told me that morning. The weak voice from the bedroom; his anxiety that he'd miss me before I went if the carer didn't finish helping him with his morning routine. The coughing and crying out in pain.

My eyes fixed upon a teasel. *Dipsacus fullonum.* I hadn't seen these before – or hadn't, up until now, noticed them; they were new to me. This plant had already flowered; the leaves had withered, the seeds set. It rose tall from the grass and tangle beside the track on a dried-out stem that broke into three, each arm topped by a seedhead the shape of an upside-down pinecone. It seemed to be holding its arms open to me.

The last thing I said to him was, *I'll see you again.*

A couple of weeks after that visit, I am sitting in my parents' flat with my mother and sister. The conversation is difficult, the atmosphere tense and drenched with sadness. I look out of the lounge window, desperate to get away from the room with all its things, the signs of their long marriage, my dad's pictures of jazz legends on the wall, the accoutrements of his illness stacked on tables. My mother has been going through photos – we want a display for the 'do' after the service – and I am disconcerted to see she's ripped up some of them, discarding them to the bin. Some have landed on the carpet; one torn square holds my blurry, teenage face. I have the urge to leap up and scrabble around at her feet, retrieve all the bits so I can piece them together.

    We are supposed to be choosing music for his service and deciding who will say what. We've already chosen the flowers for his coffin – a giant diamond of roses, Socialist red – and I have gained my mother's approbation for not wanting to see him in the chapel of rest. 'I've said my goodbyes', I tell her. Flash of the teasel on the embankment. Now she is talking about what she might do afterwards, when things are calmer. Maybe a cruise. A move. It's all going too fast. We haven't even cremated him yet, I want to say.

So I look out of the window into the cul-de-sac. Above the carpark, hanging: a kestrel.

I caught this morning morning's minion, king-
dom of daylight's dauphin, dapple-dawn-drawn Falcon, in his riding
Of the rolling level underneath him steady air...[†]

My beloved and I have stopped at a service station on the way to the Forest. It is the day before the funeral. I have practised my eulogy and co-ordinated clothing with my family (men in red ties, women in dresses, not black). The celebrant has given us an idea of what she'll say. It's all going so fast, I haven't had time to catch up. Wait, I'd wanted to say to her. That's not everything, that isn't enough. I'm having trouble remembering what is going to happen; when the service is, who is coming. My sister is organising everything funeral; my beloved and I are going to sort out Mum's financial affairs and wind up Dad's estate. I have been making lists. Lists of lists. If I could only hold these pieces in my

---

† Hopkins, Gerard Manley. 'The Windhover'.

hand, I think, if I'd only been able to write everything down on the same piece of paper, I might be able to hold it all in my head and I wouldn't lose or forget anything.

We finish our packaged sarnies and coffee, watching the desultory fountain. Feral pigeons and jackdaws haunt the paved surfaces, alert for scraps. A gull calls overhead. I have been counting red kite, as is my way, on our route west, even though there is no one to report back to now. No more boring bird reports.

There is a kestrel, hovering directly above the car. I breathe in, sharply. *I caught this morning morning's minion.*

My eldest nephew has a story about registering Dad's death. The drive takes him and my sister through the forest, up a hill. They are still quite near town, the tree cover isn't particularly deep. On the hill, a stag, head and antlers high, staring straight at the car. Humans look at stag, stag looks at humans.

It was as if... he says.

We swap these stories later, after the funeral and the 'do', when it is just the family at my sister's house, over beer and more food. I tell them about the teasel and the kestrel, me and my

superstitious, tree-hugging mind. Then Ed tells his story.
We leave a space.

My sister breaks the silence. 'He was there,' she says.

Shortly after Ted Hughes died, his friend and editor, the poet Christopher Reid, appeared at the Aldeburgh Poetry Festival. It is November, when the town smells of coal and wood smoke and the air is foggy and sharp. Under the lights, he talks about his friend and the volume of his letters he is editing – and then something detaches itself from the lighting rig and flutters down towards him. Lands on the side of his head, alights. Dances around his head, lands again. It is a butterfly, possibly a peacock, possibly a tortoiseshell – I am too far away to tell, beyond the fact that there is red and black in its colouring. The audience gives an audible gasp.

'He's here,' Christopher says.

I used to recite the opening lines from Gerard Manley Hopkins' sonnet 'The Windhover' so mockingly when I was younger. The heavy alliteration and that repetition of 'morning' seemed clumsy to me and ridiculous – perhaps because of the intensity created by those repeated sounds, when you read it aloud. But now I read the poem and I pause: 'My heart in hiding / Stirred for a bird. – the achieve of, the mastery of the thing!'

That day in the car park, my heart very firmly buttoned down beneath my layers of clothing, my composure so carefully arranged, I understood the poem's ferocity of adoration. The kestrel's pale buff underside flashed in the morning sun. It was alive. I was alive.

Maybe I imagined it, what Christopher said. But I didn't imagine the butterfly.

Bittersweet

Solanum dulcamara

The house on the corner by the wood harbours a flower with five purple petals, yellow stamens arriving at a point to make a kind of tiny tower. The plant scrambles on the front garden's brick wall, climbs over the electricity meter box. This is bittersweet: *Solanum dulcamara*, woody nightshade, gathered in April. And in the autumn, berries that ripen to a juicy, enticing red. Chop the leaves finely, poultice your cellulite. Chew the stems, taste bitter vomit, taste sweetness. Bittersweet, well-named, contains a poison that works in the blood.

The front room is illuminated in the late morning, when I pass it to enter the wood by the dogshit bin and the muddy track. A small child giggles. Waist-high growth in the garden –

not weeds, I am learning to see them as not weeds – of green alkanet and bramble. And now this curiosity, which is actually not uncommon at all, will grow almost anywhere in Britain.

I did not touch the plant. I have not poisoned myself. I push away the image of a toddler in a pram, reaching for the jelly colours, the glisten.

Blackthorn

Prunus spinosa

I am walking on the shaded track that runs between the houses
and the playing field at the bottom of Bush Wood. A number of
long-tailed tits are above me; I track their seep-seep-seep which
always sounds so carefully deliberated compared to their blue
or great cousins. Looking up, trying to catch the tiny rudders of
their tails or their 'stick-and-ball' shapes in the trees above me, I
notice the berries on a dark branch with spines. The small fruit are
purpling-black with a bloom. Sloes?

A memory darts in from a holiday with family friends,
when a walk was paused so that their mum could pick fruit from
the hedgerow. Very sour, though, she warned us. Don't try and eat
them. Her son and daughter, my sister and I, all in our teenhood,

exchanged glances and shifted about in our unsuitable footwear. The Crumblies, as we called the parents, were so embarrassing.

When they visited the next Christmas, though, she brought a bottle of purple liquid. Sloe gin! Somehow the parents didn't notice the nips we sneaked from unattended glasses. Or mind the half-glasses of blackberry wine we filched a little later. And if they noticed our slidey, blurry-eyed behaviour after that, the incoherent giggling and shouting we presented for the rest of the evening, they didn't comment. Everyone rose late the next morning. Drank a lot of tea. Quarrelled over aspirin.

Now, here at the side of this Leytonstone track; yes, sloes, fruit of the blackthorn. I imagine myself, like Carol, measuring sugar, washing fruit, sterilising jars and flagons and demijohns. Handwriting labels in beautiful calligraphy, magicking bottles of glowing purple into friends' hands. I pick a handful just in case. We have some gin at home. I could do a mini-experiment. See what happens.

Back in the house, I drop the sloes into a compartment in the fridge door and experience a moment of doubt. Are they sloes? What if they are something else? What if I poison myself? I wash my hands just in case. I check my books of wildflowers and medicinal plants to make sure. Sloes. What else can they be?

The bluish-black fruit has a surface bloom and a spherical drupe containing a small amount of greenish pulp and a large, yellow, hard stony seed.

Yes. Sloes. I wash my hands again. I can try to make sloe gin later – at the weekend perhaps. The fruit will keep.

Because it has a trunk that twists, people used to make unusual-looking walking sticks from blackthorn. There is a story from Devon recorded in *Folklore* – the journal of the UK's Folklore Society – about such a 'twisty stick', which trips its owner up and drowns her. For blackthorn has a long association with the supernatural.

As summer passes and the days get greyer and shorter, I go out less and less. I scroll through the news, I lurk on social media. I spend hours drifting from site to site on the web. Blackthorn features strongly on NeoPagan websites, often as part of an entire symbolic system based on Ogam. This early Irish writing system contains letters attributed in medieval times to individual trees (one of which is the blackthorn), although how widely or accurately this attribution can be extended to all the letters in the

Ogam alphabet has since been revised. Robert Graves made much of these attributions in *The White Goddess*, devising an entire mythological system based in part on Ogam scholarship that has since been discredited, but *The White Goddess* still exerts its pull.

Blackthorn, the websites tell me, can indeed be used for self-protection. But be careful; it's associated with the Otherworld, with death.

Cold spells in spring or early summer are Blackthorn Winters. The winter after I pick my handful passes very wet and and warm for the time of year, but it has a frozen quality all the same. By Christmas, the UK is in its second lockdown and the prospect of seeing my family and friends has disappeared. I send gift vouchers and parcels. None of them contain sloe gin.

Item 2137 in The Museum of Witchcraft and Magic's collection is described as a 'blackthorn blasting rod'. It consists of

> three blackthorn stems (cut from where a single branch divided into three stems) twisted together into a helix, and joined at the end with a short length of black tubing.

The ribbon around it is a deep red.

Item 2765 is a vial of oil, containing a single thorn; useful, according to the text label, for spells of self-protection.

Blackthorn as cordial or tonic. Blackthorn in flower, blasting out its brightness. Is it a hex or is it an invigoration?

It is spring. I have rallied after a grim few months and am walking every day. The weather has been changeable; wild winds and rains and now this mild air. I am still battling the bad thoughts, the hand-washing, the catastrophizing. The pandemic is still very much around. But I am out here at least.

Everything has burst into activity on Wanstead Flats. A wren blasts out its song, a persistent chiffchaff narrates – and there is a blackbird in the trees beside the playing fields unrolling a constant music. I have taken to walking that way in order to hear him. Crab apple blossoms, red deadnettle in abundance. Some of the newer street trees are cherries in flower. And banks of white blossom; I feel dizzy with the sound – white-tailed, buff-tailed, carder bees at their work of collection – as I try to capture the blazing flowers on my phone. They are blackthorn saplings, I realise; not mature enough to produce sloes this year, but maybe, if they aren't cleared away or caught in a fire, I might be picking a crop one day. Making that gin.

Meanwhile, here is this abundance. The dazzle, sun on blackthorn in flower; those dizzying, proliferating depths of blossom flash in my mind later, when I resume my station on the bed. The notion of bad luck has been preying on me. The sloes I picked last summer have shrivelled and puckered in the fridge compartment.

One day – I am sick of myself and my Doominator tendencies, and the prospect of seeing more of spring draws me outside – I wrench the fridge door open and scoop out the dried-up fruit. I march myself to the wood. There is a clearing there, with a pond-turned-bog, where I like to stand and mutter to myself – or actually, mutter to the surrounding trees, the crows, the parakeets. To whatever might be listening, really – I often have an unnerving and excitingly eerie sense that something is listening. As if the whole wood has suddenly turned in my direction, noticed me. So I make for the clearing, and when I reach it, I drop the sloes.

'Sorry,' I say. 'For you.'

I don't know who I'm talking to, but I picture the crows bouncing down beside my offering. Ants or beetles carrying it off. Mould or fungus colonising it. Or maybe a blackthorn seedling nosing aside the moss.

Flasher

Homo sapiens subs. *ostendit penis*

It is early morning on a Saturday in late winter and I'm out for a jog round Bush Wood, enjoying my slow but comfortable progress around the loop I've plotted out. I walk and then run, walk and run and cough a bit at the traffic fumes floating over from the junction by the Keeper's Lodge. The branches of the limes and oaks are stark against the opaque sky and I shuffle happily through leaf litter. At the bottom of my circuit, where a path joins the wood from Blake Hall Road, a young guy on a bike approaches. He looks mournful, I think, as he watches me toil past him. I catch grey jogging bottoms, mouse-coloured hair. There aren't many people about at this time. In an hour or so, the parkrunners will form a long, intermittent string, plotting their own, larger loop around the green space, but I prefer my solitary exertions and have never joined them.

I trot past saplings in a clearing – no more, really, than a space between tracks – and am about to turn towards the ex-pond-now-marsh nearby when I catch sight of a man at the side of the path ahead of me. He seems to be having a pee. Is it the cyclist? I tut and turn the other way.

The next Saturday, it is sunny and I am cheerful. The 'running' is going well. I am still slow but it is more comfortable and I settle into an easy pace. I run for a bit, then walk. And repeat. I feel a bit self-conscious running next to the road, but my middle-aged invisibility serves me well, I think. No shouted comments, at least. I turn the corner at the top of my loop to take the track that runs beside Bush Road and before I can register it, I am running past him. Cock out. Side on, beside the spreading stump of a felled, veteran chestnut. Is it the same guy as last week? He must have an awfully full bladder, I think.

Then just as swiftly. Oh. I think I have been flashed.

No sound of liquid hitting the ground anyway. I am annoyed – a woman can't even go for a run without this nonsense. And such a young guy, too. Though I'm not sure what age I'd deem appropriate for flashing. I continue on my route and at the bottom of the loop I pass the Parkrun guy, setting out the signage. Behind him, standing side on, the flasher is there, holding his dick more prominently now. I look again to be sure as I carry on towards the top of my loop. I have five minutes left before I'm finished, so I concentrate on running a bit faster, breathing a bit deeper. I reach the chestnut stump. He is there again. He must have run himself to meet me from the other side of the wood. Flasher, you shouldn't have! This time he has pulled up his dark T-shirt to cover his face, exposing his pallid belly.

'I'm calling the police,' I say over my shoulder, not breaking stride, not slowing down, speeding up, in fact. Breathing deeper. 'I know exactly what you look like.' I am fuming.

As I walk back home, I warn a couple in leggings who pass me. They ask me if I'm ok. The question takes me aback: of course I'm ok – 'just annoyed', I tell them. I say the same thing to the police officer on the phone once I'm back home. She starts talking about victim support and I say, no, I'm fine, just irritated I can't go out for a jog without this happening. They send a patrol car but see nothing.

The following Saturday, I avoid the wood, stick to the playing field instead. It has sunk in a little more; this guy was targeting me. So much for my cloak of concealment. Misogyny is never going to leave me alone. I can't retire from it, I can't rusticate and go on retreat from it. I can exploit its flipside – the one it shares with ageism – all I like, but it can flick out a tentacle any time it likes, throw me off my path, hurl me to the ground.

And if I decide to be 'robust' – I did carry on jogging around the wood after a while, but I made sure to carry a phone, with my keys stuck between my fingers like the old days – and it is rare, for me, this harrassment, what about everyone else? A few years later, a stranger tries to grab a woman and wrestle her down into the undergrowth by one of those tracks through the wood. She fights him off, the police investigate.

When I learn this, I think about that young flasher. Was it him? Did he 'escalate'? Did they catch him? Did they get him help? Has he moved on to a different wood, a different set of targets?

Common Field Grashopper

Chorthippus brunneus

It's a sunny day in early autumn. I head out again towards Bush Wood. Along the verge, between road and trees, the grasses are pale and tall, flowering. I scoop a grasshopper out of the puddle it has just landed in. It jumps off. There are runnels in the track – and on the paths under the trees, more and more tree roots have been exposed. Some day those trees will die, come down. Not today though. Today, green woodpeckers are loud – and blackcaps with their rich, excitable song.

I pause by the Keeper's Lodge on the corner beside a tangle of bramble and grass. The grating buzz of *Chorthippus brunneus* is loud here. It's one of the sounds of summer; all those heat-dazed walks on the Flats before they cut the grass, the blonde stems reflecting light, the accompaniment of grasshoppers, thousands of them, singing. I've only recently learnt to identify them and I'm keen to watch them in action. It is the male who sings first, rubbing leg against wings in a courtship performance. If a female is attracted, she will sing back to him and between them they will change the song.

The walker finds me bent over the grasses, trying to follow the progress of a large grasshopper as it negotiates the stems. We talk about local walks and how restorative they are during lockdown. A kind of meditation. Before I know it, I am being instructed; he puts down his water bottle to demonstrate. I know, I say, I am learning to meditate too. He pauses, carries on: the precise placing of the chair upon which to sit, the correct way to breathe. Oh, I try again, that's like what I have been taught, I see the parallels. He pauses again. Expression of bemusement, smiling, a question there. He carries on. I am asked what I think a leaf is. I answer evasively. I am told about science. That's choroplasty, I'm told. He loses his thread. He carries on. The intention is not courtship, but instruction. I would be irritated if it weren't so good to talk to someone, after all those months two metres apart, on our essential trips only.

Gregarious *Chorthippus brunneus*, those lovely darker brown bars on your sides. Your flaxen, greyish, tan, blonde, brown and twiggy self. It is so hard to find you in amongst the grasses. I watch for the *boing* as you leap between them or where they moved, disturbed by your ungainly crawling, disturbing them. Here till October – then where do you go, when it gets wet and cold? Eggs tucked into the soil until May. You sing one note, again and again. There are so many in this verge it seems a single, continuous buzz that pulses and rises.

Then one: an abdomen ending in a tawny orange, a brief flash caught as it moves over the unevenness of bent stems, crawls between the grasses. Adult grasshoppers live for about two months. All of them living and dying in the months I didn't go out here.

Red Kite

Milvus milvus

High up in circles above our Leytonstone garden: triangular tail and the hook of those splayed-fingertip feathers, pigeon-followed, like a Royal with an entourage. I rush outside to get a better view, colliding with the washing as I raise the binoculars to my face. Too late, and I can't see it anyway, my glasses are all smeared and I can't get the focal length right. The last time I rushed out like this was to see an old wartime bomber lumber across the sky, heading west. It was flanked by jets and followed by the Red Arrows. As the planes disappeared into the distance, I saw the trails of coloured smoke beginning.

Later, I go for a walk in Wanstead Park. A man in a wide-brimmed hat with a heavy pair of binoculars slung around his neck is training another pair of binoculars upon the waterfowl on the lake. He tells me he hasn't seen much that is interesting yet – it's summer, the migrants have departed or are yet to arrive – and so I offer up my red kite sighting from the morning. How I knew it by the tail. He is sceptical. He looks at me – no kit, no hat, no walking shoes.

But I saw it. I know that bird.

Back at home, I am vindicated: the London Birders' WIKI page reports a sighting nearby.

Dad would have been as unimpressed as my Wanstead Park birder by my sighting. I used to count the red kites I saw from the train or car window on my way to the Forest, and it became one of our routines. I'd tell him how many and where I saw the first one and he would be unimpressed, if pleased I was taking an interest. Over the years, my claims grew larger – I SAW TWENTY! WE WEREN'T EVEN AT BEACONSFIELD! – but his response was the same. Small potatoes, I guess, compared to the avia he chased on birding holidays. I never grew tired of sighting them, though; the V and the upturned ends of their wings, the forked tails, the sheer size and boldness of them.

Red kite nearly became extinct in Britain, after years of what the literature calls 'persecution' – largely due to 'hunting sports' which required the eradication of raptors from the 'estates' so that the game birds survived long enough to be shot. Sporadic attempts throughout the early twentieth century did little to reverse the decline in numbers, but in 1989 a more fully coordinated project began with the release of six red kite from Sweden in northern Scotland. Four were released in southern England – along with one Welsh kite – and the early nineties saw the release of over ninety more. By 1997, the English population was considered self-sustaining. A paper reporting the practicalities of the reintroduction scheme is vivid with detail.

Two aviaries were built half a kilometre apart on estates containing woodland and farmland. Nestlings were taken from sites in Sweden, Spain and Wales, carefully chosen at a specific stage in their development: young, but not so young that they'd imprint on their human handlers or be vulnerable to cold without their parents and nestmates. In Wales, the young birds had hatched from eggs removed to a rescue centre from nests vulnerable to egg-theft. Indeed, some of the dummy eggs their parents sat on were then stolen by the very same egg-collectors.

The kites were placed in the aviaries during May and June

and human contact was kept to an absolute minimum. They were fed with food contributed by gamekeepers or gathered as roadkill and frozen till needed; in England, this meant grey squirrels, rabbits, crows, weasels, ferrets – creatures legally trapped as part of 'game management'. Anything killed with a shotgun was avoided because of the danger of lead poisoning.

At ten to twelve weeks old, the birds were released; the paper notes with surprise their proficiency at flying, despite their early life in captivity. The doors were opened – in Scotland, this happened at dawn – and the birds were freed in groups of ten. For three or four weeks, food was dropped off regularly near the aviaries; fallow and muntjac deer and fox carcasses which had to be slit open so that the birds could bypass the tough skin. Anything smaller was carried off by individuals and didn't benefit the whole group. Initially, the red kite settled nearby, roosting in 'loose groups', and returning to the release site to feed. But as the weeks progressed, fewer and fewer came back. They dispersed in the autumn or spring and were recorded as far away as northern France and Cornwall. Many returned in winter, though about a quarter of the birds didn't survive.

And they bred. Successfully. They laid their eggs in nests high up in mature trees – in southern England, beech and oak for preference, with sycamore and white poplar also used. Sometimes the nests were built from scratch, but at other times, an old nest – kite or other raptor or even a squirrel's drey – was adapted.

The report, with all its detail, glows with care and appreciation. It concludes as follows: 'It is hoped that, by the year 2000, there will be five breeding populations in the UK, exceeding 350 breeding pairs in total.' When some of the authors reported back in 2002, they counted 430.

It is July, 2019. I am walking back from the Tube after teaching my evening class, and notice the moon; orange and crescent and huge in the depths of the sky's blue. Tonight there is a partial lunar eclipse. When I get home, I set up Dad's spotting scope in front of the back window. I see a very bright star in the middle of my view – Jupiter, to the moon's right, and there is Saturn a little nearer. A little before midnight, a star curves by on a fast trajectory: the International Space Station has made an appearance. Night of wonders! And this on the fiftieth anniversary of the lunar landing. I make a note to mention it to Dad – that'll set him off, I think. The anecdotes about 1969. The discussion of focal lengths and visibility and atmosphere.

But no, I correct myself. Not any more.

It is December, 2020, a week before Christmas. London is under Covid-19 restrictions and we are all confined to our homes except for essential trips and exercise. Hospitals report they are reaching or surpassing capacity. The virus is out there, everywhere. Autumn has declined into a warm, wet winter of flat grey skies and heavy rain and Bush Wood's tracks are mires, churned by bike tracks, running shoes, wellies, walking boots, hooves. When dawn arrives – later and later as the shortest day approaches – it offers a lid of cloud, so that the lights we switch on in the morning stay on for the rest of the day. Some days, I don't get outside at all. 'Out' is contained instead within the long oblong of the back room window, or the flash of the lime trees' yellows out the front.

In bed one morning, cereal bowl beside me on the sheets, coffee stains on the pillow where I'd lurched upright, scrolling and scrolling through the news websites, I find the word for it. I feel despair. It isn't as bleak as I'd imagined, despair. There is a heat to it, a kind of 'We're FUCKED' abandon. If the Government wants me, a herd member, to go out and catch coronavirus and die and stop burdening the NHS with my asthma and my mental health problems and my dodgy thyroid and my middle-aged uterus, then perhaps I ought to bloody well go out and catch it. For a moment, hunched over my laptop, back sodden from the latest hot flush, I feel free. I don't care what happens to me and it is a huge relief.

A day before the shortest day, I queue with my beloved outside the Tube car park for a COVID-19 test. In three days' time, the Christmas Rules will come into force and we will be allowed to travel out of London, visit family. I am terrified. I am desperate to see my folks. The queue is long, it's drizzling and cold, but the mood is good-natured; stewards give us helpful tips and tell us how long we'll have to queue. I watch their colleagues handling the test kits with litter pickers, passing them through car windows, collecting them and dropping them into large plastic bins. A woman seated in the gazebo in front of me removes a swab from her mouth and retches into a handkerchief. We have been warned it feels a bit uncomfortable.

When it is our turn, we sit opposite each other at a collapsible picnic table. We've been queueing for forty-five minutes and I'm starting to shiver. I spend a moment observing the glob of mucus I have extracted from my nose – I forgot to blow it first – and my hand hovers in the air as if to brush it away. I stop myself just in time. Behind me, one of the Council workers driving a refuse truck comes to check what is going on. Can anyone take the test, he asks. Is it free? Yes, yes, says the steward, come, it's free, it's open tomorrow. I turn around and catch the man's anxious eyes above his mask. We are all a bit terrified, I think. And clumsy and embarrassed, as we try not to gag or sneeze in front of each other.

There is a press conference in the afternoon. The Prime Minister is late, but when he arrives, it is with the news that the five-day window has been closed. London is back in lockdown.

That night, I heave Dad's spotting scope out of the cupboard and set it up in front of the back window. I feel a little surreptitious: if the neighbours see me through the window, they are going to wonder if I'm a stalker, a voyeur, a sniper, a spy. But I have discovered online that it is the year of the Great Conjunction, and I want to try to see it. I won't be counting the red kite this December in memory of Dad, but I can do this.

Every twenty years, the orbits of Saturn and Jupiter make it look as though they are right next to each other in the sky. Every four hundred years, they appear to be a mere 0.1 degrees apart – and 2021 is one of those years. It's a doubly special year because it's been eight hundred years since this Great Conjunction has happened during the night.

I turn out the overhead light, open the curtains and train

the scope – set well back from the window – on Saturn and Jupiter. Definite planet-y roundness to Jupiter, a hint of the rings maybe on Saturn. Dots strung out to one side of Jupiter that could be its moons or could be reflections in the double glazing. I curse my shit eyesight and general clumsiness with dials and equipment. I curse the light pollution, though it is an utter marvel that we see anything at all from here. There they are, the two planets, closer together in the sky than they will be for another four hundred years.

It is the shortest day. There are enormous queues of lorries in Kent, unable to leave for the continent, where so many countries have closed their borders to travellers from the UK. A new variant of the virus has emerged in London. My relative's carers confirm they will be visiting as normal at Christmas and will look after her. She doesn't answer the phone these days, so I may not get to speak to her. My *thank yous* get blurry as I start crying.

Red kites migrate in spring from Europe to the south and east of England, and young British kites have been found in Southern Europe during the winter months. Even so, most of the kites in Britain (and Wales contains half this population) stay put. Now that restrictions have lifted, I still count them when I travel down to the Forest. They are everywhere, ubiquitous as leaves, circling above roofs, wheeling over stands of trees beside the motorway.

Canalag Goose

Anser anser x Branta canadensis

It is autumn and the anxiety that makes me hover on thresholds and cancel outings still has me in its talons. My nature-watching is reduced to what I can see out of the back room window or on a screen. One evening, a local photographer posts a picture on social media, taken that day at a local pond. A goose stands by the water. Its legs are a muddy pink, its neck is dark, with white speckles and the area around its eye is white. It has a salmon-pink to orange beak. What is it? It doesn't seem to match any of the pictures in my bird book.

I am looking at a canalag; a cross between a Canada goose and a greylag (although, as I look at the unsuspecting bird side-eyeing the camera, I name it 'greynada', for I love greylag geese the best and they should always come first). They are the most common type of hybrid, though others also exist. The experts are precise and provisional in their explanations of how and why this cross-breeding happens, but 'nest parasitism' – where a female will leave an egg in another's nest – is thought to be a factor. When the gosling hatches, it imprints – and the goose family is extremely imprintable – upon whichever adult is there. Thus a greylag gosling hatched into a Canada's nest will socialise and mate readily with them. In an experiment where greylag eggs were put into Canada nests, the juveniles all went with their foster parents to the wintering grounds. When they returned, the young female foster greylags paired with other greylags, but just over a quarter of the males took Canadas as mates. When some of them lost their partner, their new partners were also Canadas.

Another possible explanation for the canalag's existence is when a male goose will force copulation upon a female outside its mating pair; ornithologists do call this 'rape' though the more official, technical term is 'forced extra-pair copulation'. Canadas are amongst the species that show this behaviour, so although it hasn't been as thoroughly researched as it has amongst ducks, it is a likely source. As well as this, hybridization might be more likely when geese are in captivity or there are few geese of the same species nearby.

Hybridization isn't a new or remarkable thing to botanists

or ornithologists. To birdwatchers, particularly devotees of the gull in all its varieties, hybridity is a familiar aspect that frequently makes identification tricky. Tim Dee, in *Landfill*, his paean to gulls and their world, is forthright: 'Gull taxonomy is messy.'

> [W]hile we fiddle over what to call their connection, the gulls are hybridising, their populations are dynamic, their ranges shifting, they are genetically and geographically active within species as well as across bird borders.

He points out that even the august *Handbook of the Birds of the World* throws up its hands when faced with the herring gull's complexities.

As taxonomy has gained in precision, right down to the genetic level, scientists are able to make finer and finer distinctions when mapping flora and fauna against their classifications. The tree branches and branches as the zoologists see more and more with their instruments. And what they see is that nature simply will not stand still. The International Ornithologists' Union is clear:

> Classifications are dynamic sets of hypotheses about population dynamics and evolutionary histories. They are subject to regular revision based on new published research, not static lists for implementation.

If classifications are *hypotheses* – that is to say, ideas based on observation and investigation, carefully and fully thought-out but for all that, tentative – then classifications have humility. They say, *we venture, we see the possible, we are open to challenge and change.* I hadn't really thought of it before, but I'm beginning to see that naming might be an act of love and hope; a tentative reaching-out for connection with the named. A kind of greeting.

Back in Leytonstone, I stare again at the picture of the canalag (greynada). It isn't aware it is remarkable. When I venture out the next day – almost at dusk, swerving off the pavement and cringing slightly whenever I pass another human being – I head for the pond on Dames Road. It feels weird to be outside and my anxiety runs high – the familiar pounding in my head, the pains in jaw and neck and shoulders – but the air is cool and I breathe in, deep, avid for the smell of wet foliage. I set my back to the road and its heavy traffic, walk away from the fumes, scan the water for the canalag. I cannot see it.

It doesn't matter. It's enough just to be here, in creaturely companionship with the birds: mute swans, moorhens, mallards, coots, Egyptian geese, the ever-present Canadas.

Greylag Goose

Anser anser

It is a chill morning, but the green spaces beyond our street have drawn me outside. I want to see some more geese and have remembered the greylag pair that used to frequent the ponds in Wanstead Park, keeping company with their Canada cousins. Their presence puzzled me, for the only other place I'd seen greylags before this was in a field bordering the Loch of Harray on Mainland, Orkney, containing a storm of honking and so many plump, grey bodies. It is their call as much as anything that I love; to my ears it is so quintessentially 'goose' in its loud and lovely unloveliness. But I love also their name. *Anser* means goose in Latin, so their taxonomic name, translated, is *Goose! Goose!* Like another of my favourites, the wren – which bears the name

Troglodytes troglodytes – the greylag is so good they named it twice.

Today, I head towards the lakes and ponds on Wanstead Flats. The largest of these was constructed in the early 1900s – possibly at the same time as our house – and named Alexandra after King Edward VII's consort. When I reach the small hills that have earned it the local name of Sandhills Pond, I hear that familiar, inelegant sound and hurry towards it. More than twenty greylags jostle with mute swans and Canadas for food thrown by a family. Maybe there are more; I've lost count as I walk past the little girls with their hands full of bread, embarrassed by my tightened throat and the surprise tears.

Greylags are the UK's only native breeding goose, but the ones I pursue around the local ponds and lakes seem to be of little interest to 'serious' birdwatchers. They used to be abundant in England until their habitat was destroyed and their numbers further diminished through 'predation', so wild Hebridean birds were released onto English gravel pits and lakes between the 1930s and the late 70s to remedy this. The venture was extremely successful, the birds adapting to their new environments so well that – in the words of the RSPB's webpage for *Anser anser* – 'the resulting flocks (often mixed with Canada geese) found around gravel pits, lakes and reservoirs all year round in southern Britain tend to be semi-tame and uninspiring.' I feel somewhat indignant on 'my' greylags' behalf; I love their solidity of body, mild feather colours, orange beaks. Because they are less numerous or noisy than the hordes of Canadas they often accompany, it is a surprise and a delight to hear them give voice.

In the early 1990s, three distinct populations were thought to exist: those based in the Outer Hebrides (considered 'native'), migrants wintering in the North of England and Scotland – and the 'introduced' or 'feral' birds. Nowadays, The Wildfowl and Wetlands Trust identifies two groups: the 'Iceland Greylag Goose', which nests in Iceland and migrates to Northern Europe (including, particularly, Northern Scotland), and the 'British Greylag Goose', which includes everything else found in the British Isles. In recent years, these two populations have been found to overlap in places such as Orkney, where that sight of a whole field of them distracted me from the archaeology I'd come to admire. This monitoring and categorisation is important and useful, for to follow where the birds go, where they nest and how many young they raise is to help map biodiversity and get a picture of the effects of human agency – a picture of the impact of reintroduction or habitat management as well as of climate change and environmental degradation. It entertains me, though, that all this careful data-gathering and recording can't keep up with their subjects. The territories overlap and merge, the birds emit their squeaky honks. They are all *Anser anser*.

Common Lime

Tilia x europaea

It is summer, and the bad thoughts and needly feelings have receded with the coming of brighter days. I brave shops and public transport. The UK's Covid-19 vaccination programme is in full swing.

Today, we are sitting in a pub on the corner of the High Road, with two halves of 'craft ale', as if made by a carpenter, and I'm griping about the language of nostalgia – the old ways this, the artisan that, the hand-made this, authentic that, the pictures of green fields and clean skies on the punnet of factory-farmed eggs – when I'm stopped mid-rant by a scent that reaches right over the traffic fumes and punctures the pub smells of beer and frying. It comes from a tree across the road – not far from the bin that caught fire a few days before, still on its side all melted and set in a black-grey puddle. Through the open doorway, penetrating the sun and wind and the traffic hauling itself around Leytonstone's one-way system: lime blossom.

I'd seen people collecting the flowers along the Avenue earlier – the rows of limes that peter out into wild rose and hawthorn on the green space between Bush Wood and the tower blocks – presumably for making lime blossom tea. It's said to be good for insomnia, as well as being full of sugar and vitamin C. According to the *Macdonald Encyclopedia of Medicinal Plants*, the flowers constitute 'the basic ingredient in certain soothing drinks for over-wrought, over-excited children' – and lime wood is used to make artists' charcoal, as well as charcoal for smoked foods. The bast – the inner layer of the tree's bark – can be spun into a fibre used to make sacking. And the blossom is loved by bees; the Avenue hums at the height of flowering.

Our street is planted with limes as well; there's one directly outside the house, knobbled from years of pollarding, slanting out of the pavement towards our bedroom window. This is the tree that aphids cluster on in summer, excreting the honeydew that drips onto parked cars below. It's for this reason that limes tend not to be planted as street trees any more, but I'm glad of ours. That perfume gushes in when you open the front door, sweet with something like a citrus edge; the soft, heart-shaped leaves, furling around each other down the stem, offer shade and beauty. Later, the bracts with their suspended spherical fruits will twizzle and fall, lazily, to the pavement – and the leaves will turn through all the shades of yellow and gold, bright in the early dusk against the trees' dark trunks. They will muffle the ground and dry to brown parchment when they drop, or form a dark mulch with rainwater, feeding the plants that grow in crevices; shepherd's purse, dandelion, green alkanet. The mosses.

The common lime is a hybrid between the small- and large-leaved limes (*Tilia cordata* and *Tilia platyphylos*, respectively). For an amateur plant-spotter like myself, the latter two can be distinguished from each other by the way their flowers hang. If they are held 'obliquely erect above the foliage' then they belong to *Tilia cordata*; if they hang below the leaves, then they are likely to be *Tilia platyphylos*. Some of the flowers point upwards on the Avenue's trees, but not all. Some, like those of our street trees', hang – and this, along with their smaller leaves, indicates that those trees are *Tilia x. europaea*, also known as *Tilia x. vulgaris Hayne*; the common lime.

It is later the same summer and flash floods have beset London twice. I am walking down the Avenue in a break between the heavy rain showers and notice that the wardens have cleared the bramble and nettle, so that it's become a boulevard, no less, with a central main strip as if for traffic, and the part between each double row of trees for pedestrians.

In postcards from the early nineteenth century, this arrangement is clearly visible and the ground that extends into the artily hazy distance is pale and bare of grass, as if strewn with sand. But now, as I look at the channels eroded into the paths, I realise that what I took for loam was humus, created by all those leaves, falling every autumn. After the rain, it has been churned up by feet and paws, hooves and wheels, to reveal the underneath. The earth seems almost sandy; fine granules of it form wavy lines like tide marks where surface water collected and ran down the slight downward slope towards the Avenue's foot.

And in those channels: pebbles, pale particles. They must come from what's underneath the leaf mulch, those beds of Boyn Hill gravel that give Wanstead Flats its name, deposited by the Thames 350,000 years ago. The gradient continues towards Stratford, a gradual incline that gives an almost imperceptible drag of gravity, enough to make walking or cycling up it feel like labour. There is, allegedly, a spring nearby, paved over now and remembered only in a street name. And now this temporary stream, a very minor intermittent river. I imagine it, stormwater running – so fast through the wood, it looks as if it's boiling – down these channels, joined by streams that run off tarmac from the temporary lakes made by the blocked and turbid gutters, always downhill, drawn towards the Lea, draining into the Thames.

Some of those Edwardian postcards name these lines of lime trees Evelyn Avenue – after John Evelyn, the diarist and writer. He was the first to use the term 'avenue' to denote such rows of trees in his 1664 work *Sylva, or a Discourse of Forest-Trees and the Propagation of Timber in His Majesty's Dominions.* He visited the area in 1683, remarking on the extensive plantings by the owner of Wanstead House, Josiah Child, and ironically, pronouncing the area to be 'a cursed, barren spot'. On Google Maps' satellite view, the limes are distinguishable from the other trees by their lighter-coloured canopies, and when I lay a ruler against the screen, the Avenue is clear: four rows cutting across the grassland, pointing straight towards the top left hand edge of the Basin, where Overton Drive begins to skirt around the top of that body of water. I know this was the original approach from the west to Wanstead House – rebuilt from a design by Colen Campbell in the Palladian style for Richard Child, one of Josiah's sons.

Avenues of trees were familiar garden and landscape features by the late seventeenth and early eighteenth century – and owners of such estates habitually extended such planting outside their own grounds. Josiah Child certainly did so. As Sarah Couch points out in her survey of the history of avenue-planting, avenues demonstrated land ownership very palpably, reaffirming both the owner's mastery over nature in general and over the particular nature falling within one's boundaries in particular. The reach of Child's grasp was measured out in rows of walnuts, chestnuts, white poplar – and likely, limes. I don't know if the trees I see are the ones he planted – I'd be surprised, for they don't look old enough – but they might be closely related.

Botanists have worked out that many of the trees in the numerous lime avenues in England and Wales fall into two distinct 'clonal types'. And within each group, the trees – whether they are the ones originally planted or their descendants – share the same, single ancestor and are genetically identical. In fact, the author of the 1992 study which discovered this goes further to say that

[b]oth clonal groups were probably originally imported from

the Netherlands and were possibly derived from ancient village trees, which in the Netherlands are usually *T. x vulgaris*.

How is this possible? By consulting sources from that period (including John Evelyn's *Sylva*), Donald Pigott discovered that 'from 1650 to 1750 lime trees were usually propagated from their sprouts, either directly or by layering.' This means that each of the 'new' saplings was a clone of the original tree. This practice was extremely widespread: 'What is remarkable is the enormous numbers of trees used, all of which seem to have been derived from very few original genetic stocks.' According to Pigott, these clones – amid stock from other sources – were still planted well into the nineteenth and early twentieth centuries – so it's just possible that the tree outside our bedroom window has its origins in a Dutch village.

The limes have their scientific names thanks to Carl Linnaeus – also known as Carolus Linnaeus, also known as Carl von Linné – who regularised and developed biology's taxonomy. He included human beings in his classification system, but never identified any individual specimens of *Homo sapiens* during his lifetime. Where other taxa have a 'type' – that is, one specimen (a single creature or plant) exemplifying the characteristics of organisms with that name – *Homo sapiens* does not. But a 1959 paper by William Stearn addresses this issue and claims that Linnaeus 'must stand as the type'. So fittingly and rather poetically, the body of Carl Linnaeus, namer of the living world, bearer of three different common names, is regarded as the type of the taxonomic class, *Homo sapiens*. Actually, more accurately, he is the lectotype, being a specimen selected after the organism was first identified. The lectotype for *Homo sapiens* is buried in Uppsala Cathedral.

Taxonomy's limits and pitfalls are present from its very beginnings. Linnaeus attempted to classify *Homo sapiens* further into *Homo sapiens europaeus, afer, asiaticus, americanus, ferus* and *monstrosus*. He believed – erroneously – that humans could be grouped into 'natural' – ie biologically-based – categories. Nor does the lectotype chosen for *Homo sapiens* in any way represent our variety, it must be said, poetic though that choice may be.

When Linnaeus' family moved from the Swedish tradition of patronymic surnames to adopt a fixed family name, the father chose the name of a tree – one which grew tall near the family home. The tree is called lind in Swedish, linden or lime in English.

Great Spotted Woodpecker

Dendrocopos major

It's hot today and I'm tired. Sleep has been difficult, my dreams full of spiders and their webs, large and bulbous bodies infesting the house. They have the striped legs and white cross markings of the European garden spider, *Araneus diadematus*.

The air is still and sticky-feeling as I enter Bush Wood. I wave away a midge and cough. The traffic on the roads seems just as heavy as it did before the pandemic; I can hear idling engines and a car horn from Bush Road nearby. As if in answer, there is a sharp knocking above me, stronger and more forceful than a tap. Something impacting on or driving itself into wood. Sure enough, when I look up into the boughs of the oak above me, I catch the black pate, white cheeks – and the beak, so pointed, sharp, as the bird drives it into fissures between the plates of bark, prising out its food. Its skull has built-in shock absorbers and its tongue can extend four centimetres beyond its bill.

The woodpecker moves higher up so that it has the tree branch between us. I walk on. Everything seems precious these days, but painfully so. The blown drift of yellow lime leaves, the scraps of diseased horse chestnut leaves, this bird that shrieks – a sound like a steam-kettle's whistle, cut off abruptly – as it flies off. Pictures of California have been all over the internet; the orange skies and blackened vegetation. And when I look at the tree's roots, they seem more exposed since the last time I came this way. The fast and heavy rain we get these days and the erosion it creates.

I am surprised by another whistle: two notes, the first higher than the second, a non-verbal *YOOHOO!* It is exactly the kind of whistle used to get the attention of one's wayward dog – or maybe a child. My father used to whistle like that at me and my sister when we were kids. He was usually carrying a plank of wood or something heavy through the garden, we'd be in his way.

I turn. It is a male cyclist in lycra, fast bearing down upon me. *Homo sapiens* subsp. *duabus rotis*. I step aside, stumbling a bit into the longer grass and brambles, as he beams – wraparound shades, acid lime and shiny yellow kit, skinny, hairy legs flashing by – and shouts *THANK YOUUUUU* as he barrels down the track.

What's wrong with Excuse Me? My question fades after him. I feel churlish, embarrassed, disgruntled.

YOOHOO! I am not a dog. I am not a child. I stomp up the track, following the rut his wheels have made in the mud.

Common Black Ant

Lasius niger

Midsummer. The new nasturtium is in the pot; I notice stems below the flowers and leaves thick with sapsuckers. An ant is heading towards them. They are being herded, milked. I'd seen this on the chives, earlier in the summer, but those plants yellowed and died. Now it is happening on these rampant climbing flowers, the cheery orange and red, the leaves like little plates.

Jean Sprackland writes about exactly this strategy of the ants in her poem 'Aphid Farm', likening the aphids to cattle. It ends with a description of their secretions – the honeydew – as 'milk of paradise', 'so abundant it runs from the leaf / and drips into the dust.' There's something so bleak about that last word. Maybe it's my doomy imagination, but its connotations with death and ruin vibrate so very strongly around it – in part because it is the last word; the end word of the poem, the last to reverberate in our reader's memory. In me it activates that terror, never far away, that I seem to live with these days: that the future contains only dust. If we're lucky, maybe ants as well.

When I remember, I try to squash the aphids, or squirt the nasturtiums with soapy water. It's supposed to repel them. But I am an intermittent, lazy and easily disheartened gardener. I remember too that blue tits are supposed to be extremely efficient at removing aphids. Squatting beside the flower bed, I hear one calling in the hazel tree. Better to leave it to the birds, I think. Let the nasturtiums take their chances with the rest of the garden.

Small, powdery heaps around holes in the ground and gaps in concrete. Ants with wings, thronging the top of a grass stem.

Eyes watering, graduating from strength to strength to neat:

vinegar, lavender oil, peppermint oil. A house spider writhes, clenching its legs in on itself, sprayed accidentally as I squirt with one hand and whack with the other. Ants have appeared in the kitchen – many of them, emerging from cracks and vents, clinging to tea towel and wall, behind the cooker, fleeing up windows and pipes. I itch all over, long after I've killed every one. Half an hour later, I return to the kitchen and have to start again. Spraying, bashing, sweeping, wiping, cleaning. Any thought of the innocence and preciousness of creaturely life has disappeared.

Later that evening, I feel a tickle on my arm – and there is an ant, watching TV with me, negotiating hairs.

Last year, cutting back some grass at the edge of our concrete patio, I lifted a piece of turf to uncover neat white clusters of tiny ovoids. A single ant with an egg in its – what, its jaws? its forelimbs? I couldn't see too clearly – turned this way and that, as if unsure of the safest direction, or unwilling to abandon all its charges. I replaced the turf, excited to have encountered this uncommon sight. Now, as I wipe and bash and spray, I recall that moment with grim rage. I should've brought a boiling kettle from the kitchen, poured it over.

I see the writhing abdomens tucking in towards the thorax, the clenching inwards of legs, the bedraggled crawling away and I do not care. I shudder against the feeling of crawl on my skin, the prickle of its raised hairs. Tiny, alien, too numerous, unwelcome.

They will build their nests underground, close to houses for warmth. They do not mind gravity, are easily oriented wherever their heads are pointed. They speed-crawl everywhere; antennae wave from the top of the blinds, cupboards, on cloths intended to wipe them from existence. They blunder into my hair, they delicate-dance across a bare foot. They cling to the scrubbing brush, rest in the folds of curtains.

We break. We borrow some ant killer from our neighbours – a weird, amber gel you inject into cavities. They bought it on the internet. We wonder if it is legal. We think of bees and spiders. We inject it anyway.

They're gone.

Honeysuckle

Lonicera periclymenum

I am running. To dignify it with that word captures none of the staggering, the roughly on-the-spot stumble, the rasping breath and sweaty dishevelment of it, the dizzy astounded *I'm-up-at-what-o'clock?* of it. So it is with some relief that I am distracted every time I pass this point on my circuit by a scent that swarms around my own stink of sweat-and-coffee-breath; distractingly strong, intensely sweet. It is like lime blossom, but with far less citrus, far more cloves – in fact, the more I turn my attention to the smell, the more the clove undertow sucks at me as I pad slowly away. I crane my neck but can't see it.

I labour along the path. The break between bursts of running is gasping relief. Still, even moving as slowly and untidily as this, I can enjoy the limbs swinging and the deep breathing. I'm so preoccupied with catching my breath and not stopping that I reach that place on the path again before I realise it. The smell is like jasmine but without the sickliness. Wholly different to sweet chestnut in flower, which smells savoury, like mushroom or sex. Neither lime trees nor jasmine nor indeed *Castanea sativa* are in flower yet, though I know where they are, and I know it won't be long.

Third circuit, nearly finished. I slow down to a walk, take a puff of my inhaler. That I'm out here at all, able to exercise, feels miraculous. Since the pandemic began, I've had trouble stepping out of the house. When the honeysuckle finds me, I have been limiting myself to the odd run and the occasional, anxious errand to pick up prescriptions. The whole of Leytonstone, it seems, is taking to the woods and the playing fields, the parks and open spaces and I have been getting up earlier and earlier to find a time when I can keep my distance from my fellow exercisers.

That scent again. This time, I leave the track, picking my way through ivy and bramble under the oaks. There. *Lonicera periclymenum*, pale cream and yellow, so thick-flowering I doubt it really is honeysuckle. It is concealed behind the trees that border the bridleway along which I run, visible now as snatches of pallor behind the oaks and holly, growing profusely along the boundary with the Quakers' Meeting House – there must be a wall under all that greenery. Bees are loud around it.

It is the first time I have encountered it here. All the years I'd been walking this path, honeysuckle has been proliferating, climbing over itself, over bricks. Harrap's tells me it is a 'deciduous climber', the 'older stems woody, with peeling bark', 'younger shoots purplish' – and that the flowers are 'very fragrant, especially in evening.'

I am greedy for it. Greedy for wind and leaf music, for the birds that arrow across my path, the clapping-two-stones-together of the blackcap's alarm call, its squeakily fruity song. Parakeets like a sensor alarm shrieking, a green woodpecker's heckle. This abundance of thriving blossoming, hysterical scent.

The following summer I am still stumbling around Bush Wood at odd hours in a bid to avoid people. A mixture of embarrassment (I still cannot run continuously for thirty minutes, I still rasp like a heavy smoker) and fear drives me. It isn't rational – so many of us have been double-vaccinated and boosted, it is clear that being outside vastly reduces the risk of Covid-19 infection – but I'm picking my battles when it comes to challenging avoidant behaviour.

I remember the honeysuckle, the way it draped so abundantly over the brick, the smell of it everywhere – and pick the path that takes me past the site. At first, I think that someone's got round to weeding and pruning in the Quakers' garden and the honeysuckle's gone, but as I get closer, I see the familiar oval leaves and the upturned crown shape of the flowers. There aren't many, and they aren't open. What I thought was a wall is in fact a series of saplings, completely swamped by the climber and as I look at the ground cover, I pick out its tendrils and spread. It seems to be everywhere in this thicket; honeysuckle as festoon, honeysuckle as carpet, smothering the ivy, obdurately unblooming.

Although honeysuckle's berries are poisonous, the flowers and leaves are not. Butterflies and moths as well as bees feed on it, particularly the white admiral butterfly, which is in severe decline. The pied flycatcher makes its nest of honeysuckle bark, as does the dormouse. The plant contains tannins and sugars – and salicylic acid, the same substance as in willow, from which aspirin is derived. Culpepper used it in a conserve as a remedy for asthma. And honeysuckle has a place in folklore; it protects cattle from witchcraft. It symbolises faithfulness and love.

It was so abundant last year. What is different? What will the insects do now?

Loiterer

Homo sapiens subs. *cessator*

I'm sitting at a café table at Stratford station, waiting for a train to take me east, to the university where I teach a weekly poetry workshop. This is Stratford-atte-Bowe, as it used to be called, rather than the Stratford of William Shakespeare. On a walkway above the main concourse, a group of boys is giggling together by the glass safety barrier. One of them leans forward over it; another makes as if to run away from the group. Below them, the stream of travellers intent on catching their trains and getting to work hardly look up.

What are they doing? I watch them more closely. An opaque drop falls from the leaner's mouth, catching the light on its descent. I look away. He is spitting on the commuters. Now a Transport for

London employee has appeared, making stately progress towards the teenagers. They catch sight of him, disperse, move on.

The next day back at home is bright, gold, inviting. I set out for my daily walk, giving a wide berth to a young couple walking down our street with a wicker basket between them. The man wears a straw hat, the woman is in a sundress. They're heading for the playing field at the end of our road – popular for picnics, especially since the pandemic. There are rugs, bottles of wine. I think about Grace Dent's wry observation:

> "Picnicking" is what we're now calling getting pie-eyed in the park if you're wearing a Boden frock [...] if you're wearing a stained tracksuit, you're still officially a "street-drinker".

It is busy in Bush Wood as well, so I take a route around its perimeter. I find myself walking through the grassy area between the Quakers' Centre wall and the road. I haven't really paid much attention to this space before; it's just an interim bit of land you pass over on the way to the wood or the houses, criss-crossed by desire paths. But following one of those paths through the patchy grass, with the sun picking out leaves, I realise it is rather beautiful. There are three crab and one apple tree, blossoming. Wild cherry, blackthorn and elder amid the field maple against the boundary wall. A posse of six squirrel kittens fuss and chase each other around the large horse chestnut that stands sentinel to the entrance of the wood; I stop and listen to their scratchy huffings, the sound of claw scrabble on bark. Two butterflies weave shaky circles around each other above the brambles which are partly in flower, partly in fruit.

It is a pastoral idyll, I think. Idyll, from the Latin word *idyllium*, taken in turn from the diminutive form of a Greek word meaning 'a small picture' and originating in Theocritus's short, poetic *Idylls* of the early third century BCE. Literary idylls are rural or pastoral poems that feature landscape strongly and we use 'idyllic' nowadays to mean beautiful, peaceful, pleasant, to indicate a moment or a place that has these qualities. I place a frame around this moment, pausing by the apple tree, noticing, yes, apples swelling on the branches of this feral orchard.

But idylls aren't just for spaces like this, edging away from the sunken roundabout at the top of the High Road towards the Flats and the parks, linking the suburbs proper with Inner London. They are everywhere in this city. Office workers on their lunchbreak in the summer, the students throwing a frisbee in Gordon Square; the *otium* offered by London's parks and squares. *Otium*, like *idyll*, is another of those words used in discussions of pastoral literature. It describes moments of leisure, or the pleasure of retirement from public, working life – and those moments are all around us. Teenagers hanging out together on a bench in a shopping precinct after school. Smokers leaning on the railings over the water at Canary Wharf. Children and their carers beside the fountains at Somerset House or Russell Square Gardens or Queen Elizabeth II Park or Granary Square. Where there's an open or public space, an opportunity presented by the city's structure, humans will linger.

Of course, many people have no choice. The tents at the edge of the playing field at the end of the road, or under the raised service route to the shopping centre at Stratford. The cardboard pallet and duvet at the top of the Underground entrance. These 'features' of the urban environment represent very real lives in very real difficulty. And here is the danger of viewing the city through the pastoral lens: like the stylizations of pastoral literature, with its shepherdesses and snowy flocks, it aestheticizes and smooths over.

Whether a necessity or leisure choice, the urban pastoral is at risk. I'm thinking here of what is often called 'defensive architecture' (and 'hostile architecture' by its opponents); urban design which features spikes installed on low windowsills or under overpasses. Pigeon-spikes above, people-spikes below. Or the seat dividers that have appeared on some park benches to prevent people lying down to sleep – and which also, as a side effect, have prevented others from being able to use them as actual seats.

Then there is the Mosquito anti-loitering device, which emits an intermittent tone at frequencies that humans find unpleasant in order to discourage people from lingering. It has a youth-only setting with tones in the higher bands that only people under twenty-five can generally hear. The London Borough of Camden announced it was installing such a device in 2020 near Parliament Hill Lido, to deter the groups observed 'loitering' outside after dark. The legality of such devices has been debated in Parliament and criticised by human rights groups as discriminatory – but the things continue to be installed.

Who gets to loiter? When is a picnic a gathering to be dispersed? Where can you be, if you are not shopping or working in this city? These questions have resurfaced intensely in recent years. The spaces where we are free to lounge and do nothing, without spending money, are becoming scarcer and more surveilled. A fox, familiar and ubiquitous, canters across a road to duck between the railings of a gated park. A rat scuttles from under cover. Like them, we are becoming contingent to our own city. As unconsumers and unworkers we are becoming more and more unwelcome, more and more unpermitted. Maybe everyone will be classed a loiterer, one day. Maybe the Idylls of London will no longer be permitted.

A few days after watching the spitting boys of Stratford, I am leaning on a balcony myself, looking out over traffic at the Thames. It is almost autumn, still warm. I have some time before I'm due to teach my class across the river and am idling with a coffee at Somerset House. I drift back through the lobby, drawn by noise and the brightness of the courtyard on the other side of the building. I have brought just myself to this place and I sit down self-consciously at the edge of the pale square, shaded from the sun, enjoying the vista. It is a moment of *otium*, shared with all the other loiterers, including a school group.

> The fountains mark the hour with their pavanne
> of rising, falling plumes that offer, withdraw
> and court the eyes. What can we do but succumb?
> And so a group of children fizz and scream
> and then are running between, sitting on
> the jets with heavy t-shirts, rat-tailed hair.
> The smallest watches the big ones from the edge
> and holds his rolled-up trousers from his legs –
> and now the towels: a different colour for each child.
> Turquoise pokes her sodden foot into Emerald's back,
> Purple runs about in Spiderman pants.

Yellow jumps and shivers – *Where's your T-shirt?* –
drops his sandwich.

                World of flagstones, water,
warmth, reflections; how you flash alive
and hold us in connection – until the quarter
chimes, the jets subside and we disperse.

Formerly a car park for the Inland Revenue Service, Somerset House Fountain Court was redeveloped in the late nineties as a flexible space, open to the public in the day and hosting programmed events in the evening. Fifty-five jets – eleven rows of five – comprise the fountain in the centre of the court, which can be partially or completely turned off as required. The water can shoot up to six metres and is programmed to, well, *dance*.

A stray leaf from the London planes rattles in the gutter. A pied wagtail darts in a jerky sprint to the wet cobbles, veers away from the spray, dips its tail. The water hushes its music.

Muntjac Deer

Muntiacus reevesi

i

Turning: a corner past holly and bramble, within four feet of the
beast, not a dog, though it is that size.*

Backing off: weight transferred from front foot as it shoots me a
side eye, moves for the bushes. Behind which, the road.†

Walking away: fast, quiet. Inward seeing of its head jerking up, the

---

* Reeves' muntjac are feral, having been introduced into Britain in the 19th and 20th centuries from
their natural habitats in south-east China. When frightened or vexed, they emit a barking sound.
A pair were sent to London Zoo in 1838 and so the species was named in English after the man
who donated them. As if they were a pair of shoes. A pair of vases.
† In the late 1800s, London Zoo made a practice of selling them to 'collections', such as the one
owned by the 11th Duke of Bedford at Woburn Abbey in Bedfordshire. Numerous muntjacs were
released around England during the following century. This to establish populations that could
be hunted.

white and then the brown pupil within the eye.[‡]

ii

Standing: at the foot of the track, this time, muntjac thirty metres or so ahead, nose to the ground.[§]

Seeing: this briefly is enough.[¶]

Forfeiting: approaching, following. Human privileges. Undeserved.

Leaving: the way I came, holding muntjac-nose-to-the-ground like a candle.

[‡] They have 'tusks' – really, these are extra-long canine teeth – and the male has a V-shape on its forehead, with two small, backswept horns, no more than five inches long. The female has hair tufts instead.

[§] Some male muntjacs leave their birthplace well before their antlers come through, well even before their pedicles are developed. Some females stay put in areas overlapping with those of their mothers. All may leave for new territories after a number of years. They have been found up to 22 kilometres away from their original sites. They are adaptable, early to mature, solitary by nature, hard to detect until established.

[¶] They need bushes and tall grass for cover; bramble, nettle, bracken. They eat leaves, berries, fungi, nuts, some grasses. They will adopt territories consisting of residential gardens, especially if a cemetery is nearby. Dispersal may occur via railway embankments. They are considered invasive.

Bluebell

Hyacinthoides non-scripta, H. hispanica, H. x. massartiana

I can date pretty accurately my curiosity about urban flora and fauna, because it was the year my friend Tara died.

We'd met at a tutor's party on our first day at university. I stood by the drinks table, wondering how to do this thing called 'socialising' and watching a woman in a navy dress twist her long red hair around an index finger. She looked a bit bored, despite the lively chat and laughter around her. That, I thought, is a proper Cambridge undergraduate. I'll never get to be friends with someone like her – but I was wrong. Our friendship endured throughout university and into that fractious first year out in the world, and through all our moves to Sheffield and Camden and Kilburn, Rickmansworth, Mossley, Glossop (her) and – less further afield – West, North-West and East London (me).

We Interrailed with Rachel, the other member of our coven-triumvirate, drinking apple blossom tea by the Bosphorous, fencing with baguettes outside the Doge's Palace and fending off the men of Europe (a dick placed in the cleft of my buttocks on a Florentine bus, a hand tapping Tara's arse on a Parisian pavement). We holidayed in Ibiza together, getting sunburnt and drunk in the heat and dazzle of San Antonio. At home, wherever that was at the time, we'd stretch out with our wine or coffee in her room that smelt of incense and cigarettes and we'd listen to music and talk – about being women, about what that seemed to mean to the world and what it actually meant to us. And then there would be silences, safe silences, with both of us listening.

Later, when she and her partner Simon had moved into the flat in Kilburn, they'd take me to pubs where you could get a pint of lager for less than a quid and we'd talk about music, about the bands they were meeting through their promotions work, about drama and life and everything in that way you do when you're young and have so much time but feel like you have none. I was a schoolteacher by then, exhausted by my own relentless perfectionism and the scraping grind of early starts and heavy workloads. No time for discovering the daytime city those years; my landscape was the grey of pavements and early morning starts, the suburban Vegas of Christmas lights at the end of term, border roses edging front gardens converted into car parks. It was roundabouts and pelican crossings and the muddy grass of playing fields.

But London was also a dizzy, orange labyrinth cracking itself open at night: the roads we barrelled down in Simon's car, the rooms and corridors under and behind auditoria and stages, the crash barriers that separated out the queueing punters and on which we lolled. The little venues and the security guys who worked them, who lifted up the rope or inched open the door for us and our boxes. Coin clattering into the float tin, the stutter and howl of sound checks. I helped Simon and Tara sometimes with their music promotions work when they were short-handed; a few hours handing out ephemera or putting up posters, and you got to see the gig for free. The city's night face figures in my memory as a series of venues: the Brixton Academy, the Forum, the Garage, the Palace, the Apollo, the Dublin Castle, the Good Mixer, the Water Rats, the Astoria. Its day face was the flash of opaque sky before the Tube tunnel, the suburbs where I tried to hold the interest of teens in institutional buildings that were either freezing or stifling. At the end of the day, gulls and pied wagtails lifted off from puddles in tarmac as the school doors broke open and the kids in uniform came out, the backdrop rattle of train carriages obscured for a while by their din.

I left school-teaching after about ten years. It was the best and worst job I've ever done. On one of my last days, I looked up at the flock of starlings pinging and chuntering on a building's array of masts beside the A12. They were free, as I soon would be. As I watched, the flock – a murmuration – took off, to bell out into the paling sky.

Tara died on a night when the Perseids crossed the sky and London sweltered under the cloud that hid them. I realised I'd failed again to see them make their annual crossing as I cleaned my teeth. I nodded at myself in the bathroom mirror: Next year, I'd try and see them then. And I would definitely remember to text Tara in the morning, tell her that yes, we could meet her on Tuesday in Greenwich, that I wanted to take some pics of us, and of her and Simon and Eden all together.

But that morning Simon phoned us: Tara had suffered a heart attack and didn't survive.

The last time I saw her, it was early spring in Norwich. I was recovering from a nasty virus and still feeling odd, sounding hoarse: our conversation swam in and out of the caff's chatter and I had trouble holding onto it. Rachel was there as well and we ate veggie food and cackled at each other's jokes and I whinged about the PhD I was doing, about feeling isolated and anxious. My friends were kind and funny and supportive. If I'd known how little time we three had left together, I might not have wasted it on all the self-flagellation and complaining. Tara seemed happy: still in love, and with her daughter doing well, and working freelance so that she could scale the business up and down as needed. She was frustrated too: child-care is hard work and so is running a business, and so is juggling, and she had so much she wanted to do. But life seemed good.

Then it was time to leave, knocking back the last of the wine, swapping wooden benches and fairy lights for the opaque sky, the raw air. We said goodbye on a street corner; grey pavement and iron-hard, East Anglian cold, buses, all of us hugging and wishing we had more time, promising to get together more often. I bounced away, feeling a little more substantial, a bit more capable. She had that effect on me, Tara.

Her name means 'Queen' in Irish Gaelic. And in Sanskrit, star.

Her friendship was as fundamental to me as breathing and then she was gone.

After the phone call with Simon – brave, cracked voice as he trawled through the list of people he had to tell – and telling my beloved and the inert hours of shock and comforting each other, I called Rachel – and then I went for a walk. I couldn't think of what else to do. I trod the path through Bush Wood onto the pavements the other side and on to Wanstead Park. It was, I think, a beautiful day; I remember squinting in the glare and heat. Being a Sunday, everyone was out and about. I couldn't understand why they all looked so fucking happy. I kept passing women in groups of three: young women, our former selves; older women, the trio we'd never be now. I was distracted from this wretchedness by my mobile. Rachel: she was going up to Glossop, now, to be with Simon – did I want to come? I stared at the path, the cracked earth where the rains had eroded channels, exposing roots and pebbles, and the heat had dried the mud into peaks and plates. I couldn't answer.

I didn't go.

In the weeks that followed, that impasse prevailed. I couldn't write, or even – much – talk. I was raw to the world and rawly in relationship with the world – for where else could Tara be, if her body was no longer animate, if she no longer walked her daughter home from school in Glossop or bantered in the kitchen with her partner? For me, she was here. She was in the walk between our street and Michael Road, which held in its pavements the heatwave of 2004 and our footfall as we sweated and cursed our way to meet

Rachel. She was here in the house, at our pen-stained dining table, cackling and pouring herself more wine. She was in the sound of wind through dying leaves in this exhausted London August of heat and daze and not-sleeping, of red and purple around my eyes and my blocked nose and crying, crying all over the place. Crying in Superdrug because their pink plastic bags and star symbol reminded me of her, Queen of Superdrug, patron of vegan toiletries. Crying in the back room. Crying on the longer and longer walks I took because I couldn't think of anything else to do, because sitting still was unbearable – and writing, which had always accompanied me through difficult times, was unthinkable.

It was the last year of funding for my PhD. I was supposed to be writing a chapter of my critical study, but I couldn't concentrate – and the poetry, no, I felt sick and weak and unequal to any of it. What the hell could I say? I looked at my folders of notes, I opened documents and stared at the screen. I crumpled up sheets of paper, I shut down my laptop. After a week or so, I didn't even do that. It was futile. Who gave a shit? What did any of it matter now?

I could at least walk, though, and so I did, for hours and hours, in the park and by the roundabout, along the edge of the rec and through the small wood at the end of our street, beside the pond and around the tea hut, over and over in loops and circles, one foot and then another until hunger or thirst or tiredness made me head home.

Or until I saw something that stopped me in my tracks.

She was here. On the footpath before me, one of those tired days, swishing a tail like a flag of pampas grass: a long-haired cat with tawny markings, advancing towards me, vocal. Greeting my hand with its head, winding firm about my legs, purring. As if she had been waiting for me all this while, as if she had heard my supplications, half-disbelieving, to the ache-blue sky, the horse chestnuts surrounded by their dropped-too-early leaves. I had carried this grieving for so long – a cramp in my throat and my chest that felt as if it would tighten until it choked me and then tighten some more, until it dragged my lungs and muscle, my ribs and fat and skin inwards, down into a pinhole singularity of vacuum nothingness – but it eased as the cat flopped onto the gravel, stretched and ramped up its purring.

After a while, I straightened up – the cat winding still around my legs – and brushed the hair from my jeans, wiped my nose and my face and my eyes. I felt comforted. *Thank you, sweetheart*, I said. *Oh thank you. But not on my account.* And I carried on my way, my constant looping walks, leaving her sitting in the middle of the path.

The walks continued, all through August, into September, and I continued to talk to the trees in the wind, the sky, to the birds calling. The world seemed animate, responsive and as I walked, my fellow inhabitants of the world – the birds and animals and plants and people, the built things and the grown things, the still things and the moving things; all the things that persisted despite the fact that Tara had died, despite the fact that they too, like me, like us all, would end – started to catch my attention for themselves, in their own right.

I found myself one day crouched over a plant jutting from the wall of a boarded-up house. I knew this plant, I saw it everywhere. What was it? I looked it up on the internet: green alkanet. A weed, with a name you could trace back to Old Arabic. Once I knew what it was, I saw the stuff everywhere; blatant in plain sight, a retort to the rule of tarmac and brick and concrete.

The flowers were intensely blue, with a centre composed of a starry white pupil and tiny, black iris. They seemed to stare like eyes. Their gaze everywhere. The plant grew, budded, flowered and the eyes at the heart of the blue petals confronted me; impassive as death, relentless as life which dragged me, every day, further and further from Tara, stuck as she was now on one page of the calendar.

I went to wildflower books. Green alkanet started out in

the UK as a garden plant, some time before 1700, but botanists were noting it as a wild plant in south-western Europe by 1724. It's mostly a weed to gardeners these days; it's usually found near conurbations, where we've uprooted and chucked it out. Road verges, the edge of woods, waste ground. Like a lot of the plants I've become interested in, it's feral.

I started paying attention. I learnt more plant names: tansy, which I found later that summer near the spot where I had taken Rachel's call, marsh pennywort and water mint at the edge of a partly-drained pond, herb robert in the meagre square of earth around street trees. I watched more closely the creatures I saw: feral pigeons drinking from puddles, speckled wood butterflies tumble-duelling, flying ants swarming around pavement cracks. Summer faded into autumn, I weathered Tara's funeral and ashes ceremony, the year turned without her. I still wasn't writing, beyond a few, abject notes and hurried paragraphs and sat before my supervisors apologetically with little to add to our meetings. I stopped attending the seminars I'd so enjoyed before.

But I kept walking, kept noting things down: garlic mustard, herb paris, the different kinds of cresses. Sweet chestnut and horse chestnut. The rogue cyclamen that someone might have planted under the avenue of lime trees. When March came around – Tara's birthday month – I learnt that the strap-like leaves and stalks under trees and on the verges of the bridleways and tracks and desire lines in Bushwood were bluebells.

Bluebells draw visitors to woods to flood their social media with blue, and have a kind of prettiness that's on the verge of being 'twee' or 'kitsch', presenting a version of 'Nature' that is more tea cosy and kiddies' walks than hikes up remote mountains or encounters with snow leopards. There is for example, a Bluebell Fairy, with his own poem, in Cicely Mary Barker's vast collection of Flower Fairies. Barker, who was influenced by Pre-Raphaelite artists – particularly Edward Burne-Jones and John Everett Millais – and the Victorian enthusiasm for the Fae, creates in the Bluebell Fairy a 'peerless Woodland King'. Although the accompanying illustration shows a child who positions his feet and arms in a stance I might read as 'winsome' or 'cute', the verse attaches 'splendour' and strength to the fairy. He rules the woods through sheer numbers, commanding a 'hundred thousand bells of blue', the stems of which 'are tall and straight and strong', and conferring 'pride' upon the children who pick the flowers. No concerns here about denuding the landscape. Certainly no mention of the Countryside Code.

There is a familiar opposition in this poem of city against country, of health and beauty against the 'ugly streets' out of which 'the children throng'; an opposition that figures largely in pastoral literature and indeed, still, in the nature writing which has so burgeoned in British publishing in the last decades. Yet bluebells are often not so very far from the 'ugly streets' as Barker would have, with her contrast of street against wood, urban disfigurement against natural beauty. Indeed, as Carol Scott observes in her appreciation of Barker's illustrations, for all the botanical observation, this 'harmonious world where nature and human nature are in concert' is literally fantastical, because it's 'sentimental rather than real'. Scott points out the inventiveness with which the plants' different parts have been separated out and adapted to provide the fairies' clothing in the artwork, as if they were costumes for a theatrical performance. The children-fairies may resemble real children, but their context is not natural or everyday.

My own first encounters with bluebells were in an urban wood, in a suburb of Swansea. I have a black and white photo to prove it, frayed furry around the pinhole where it was fastened to a series of walls throughout my twenties. It was taken on an overcast day in Killay Woods, when my parents had taken my sister and I out for a walk. I look about five.

We are not exactly fairies. We're definitely not the Cicely Mary Barker kind of fairies. My sister's jumper is too big for her and bunches at the armholes and elbows. She is in the middle of saying something, snapped with her mouth open, mid-vowel. I am proffering a fistful of bluebells, eyes caught in the act of blinking, cheeks puffed out in a closed-mouth smile. My arm is held out stiffly, hyperextension lending it an odd bend, like a sapling trunk curving towards light. My dress is a little too short and my white knee-high socks are wrinkling and falling down, my hair dishevelled and slipping out of its bunches. I can still feel that checked shift – tan, cream and blue diamonds – tug at my armpits as it hitches up to my knickerline. I'm wearing Start-Rite shoes in my favourite colour, blue, my sister's are red. I am immersed in abundance, the sappy smell of snapped stalks, the bruised leaves as strong and pliable as the leather upon my feet. The flowers seem a bit disappointing, so curved inwards upon themselves, so few on the stalk, but their blue is as deep as I could wish, and there are so many around us. My father calls my name and I straighten and turn to him. I thought he wanted the bluebells, I hold out my gift of squashed stems and bruised flowers, but he has the camera up to his face instead, and he steps back to get us in focus. We are two ordinary little girls in a suburban wood, a patch of unused land wedged between housing estates and new-build bungalows. We stare out of the 1970s, when pollution and species extinction were not regular news items, and grip the flowers we picked.

The photo is not a clear one. The day was overcast and there's little contrast. The years of being pinned to walls has faded it, so that a quick glance merely yields a barely-differentiated sludge of grey. But if I really scrutinise the image, I'd say the flowers, with their curved stalks and pendulous flowers, are probably the so-called British native, *Hyacinthoides non-scripta*.

The large park near my home has an official 'Bluebell Wood' that is filled with people posing for their selfies when it flowers. My smaller, local wood – the one a few minutes' walk from my front door – also has bluebells. Confusingly, not all the flowers appear the same. There are a few clumps where the stalks curve over as if in imitation of the fern croziers emerging around them, and the flowers are curly-edged and deep blue, almost purple. But the others push out from their stems, are paler, more trumpet-like, with fewer frills – and these are the plants that seem to make up a lot of Bush Wood's bluebell population. What are they?

In this country, identifying a bluebell can be tricky because of the interbreeding that has occurred between the British native and the Spanish bluebell. The latter was originally imported to British garden centres as an alternative to the British native, so that we wouldn't be tempted to uproot bulbs from the wild, or pick armfuls of the flowers in the woods, and could enjoy a bluebell in our own gardens without damage to native stock. But *Hyacinthoides hispanica* not only escaped the bounds of those gardens – as plants do – but cross-bred with the British *Hyacinthoides non-scripta* to create a fertile hybrid, *Hyacinthoides x. massartiana*.

The spread of this hybrid has raised concerns about the extinction of the British native, as well as providing plant experts opportunities to investigate how species develop in these Anthropocene times. One such investigation in 2016 even recruited the public, inviting them to become 'citizen scientists' and send in pictures of any bluebells they saw.

And as part of the wider project investigating what is going on between *H. non-scripta* (the 'British native') and *H. hispanica (Mill.) Rothm* (the non-native), a 2010 study set out to disentangle the bluebell genus' different strands and to map their relationships. Researchers identified twelve different kinds of bluebell, using DNA analysis to establish relationships between the various taxa as closely as possible, and overturning the Eurocentricity of earlier studies by including in their investigation North African plants, where great variety can be found. The flower we know as the British native bluebell probably spread north and east from the top of the Iberian Peninsula at that point in Earth's history when the glaciers receded. It's the only taxon to have come this far north 'naturally', by which I mean without the intervention – deliberate or otherwise – of human beings.

One of the questions the study was not able to answer was whether the hybridisation was relatively recent or ancient. In the mountain ranges of central Spain, the two taxa exist side by side, one apparently having evolved out of and then flourished alongside the other, but distinguishing between them has proved difficult. There is even debate over whether the 'Spanish bluebell' identified in British handbooks is the one identified in the study. Nevertheless, its authors point to the ease with which the two taxa interbreed in Britain and theorise that they are therefore sisters.

This brings me straight back to those bluebells in Bush Wood, and my difficulty in identifying them as native, hybrid or Spanish. It isn't just my newness to the lexicon of taxon, clade, sepal and anther that is causing this: taxonomy's exactness may always eventually fray in the face of nature's adaptability. Classification systems – any system, actually – are too perfectly segmented to account for the messy fluidity of life in the material world.

Confusion about which bluebell we are actually looking at – and what to call it – seems part and parcel of our relationship with this plant, which has gone through at least three different scientific names, sometimes used concurrently, since its first identification. As with so many plants, its name is drawn from Classical myths as well as language: *non-scripta* means 'unlettered'. This is a reference to the story of Apollo and Hyacinth, a young man beloved by the sun god and accidentally killed by him.

Apollo, god of a complicated list of things, including knowledge, prophecy, disease and healing as well as the sun, is also the god of poetry and music and singing. He is reputed to be the father of Orpheus with Calliope, the muse of epic poetry, who gave her son his verses – and in Ovid's *Metamorphoses*, Orpheus sings of his father and Hyacinthus. Apollo and his beloved are taking turns at throwing a discus and Hyacinthus, impatient for his turn, is struck in the face by Apollo's throw. A sudden, freakish death, that shouldn't have happened. All Apollo's art cannot bring him back to life:

> Just as violets in a garden, or stiff poppies or lilies with clustering yellow stamens, once their stems are broken, no longer stand erect but, drooping, let their withered tops hang down and, with lowered heads, gaze upon the ground, so did the head of the dying Hyacinthus droop. His neck, drained of its strength, was a burden to itself and sank down upon his shoulders.

I love how the description of Hyacinthus' death prefigures his transformation. For Apollo works his art so that his beloved will live forever:

> [T]he blood which had flowed to the ground, and stained the grass, ceased to be blood, and a flower brighter than Tyrian purple grew up and took on the shape of a lily: but it was purple in colour, where lilies are silvery white. Phoebus was responsible for so honouring Hyacinthus, by changing him into a flower; not content with that, he himself inscribed his own grief upon the petals, and the hyacinth bears the mournful letters AI AI [alas] marked upon it.

Martyn Rix suggests that the flower so marked is the wild gladiolus, which has markings on three lower petals. Not the bluebell then, which has petals somewhat like a lily's but is *non-scripta* – unwritten-on, unblemished by the AIAI that distinguishes the other flower it so resembles. That flower is scarred by the force of a god's grief, brought into Apollo's realm of language and culture by those marks which mark in their turn the death of a young man, royalty, beloved of him.

When I discover this story behind the bluebell's name, it gives me pause. In its tangling of language and grief and nature it seems to find an echo in my own experience. Grief made me lose poetry and writing and talking for a while, but in its place I discovered a flower. I discovered another discourse – taxa and genera, stamen and pistils – and it let me speak again. Differently, of course, for how could it be otherwise?

When the bluebells come around in Bushwood these days, I stop to think about Tara. In the first few years after her death, I kept a tally of how long it had been. Rachel and Simon and I; we would tell each other the amount of time since Tara had been alive and her absence still seemed impossible, despite the mark it had left on us. We looked so tired, so battered. I let the dye leach from my hair and didn't replace it, Simon was weighted by the trudge of living without her in the house they'd shared, the work of raising their child alone.

As I write this, it's been nine years, one month. I don't count the days anymore. I had to pause to count the time gone before typing it in; life has dragged me onwards and somewhere along the way my sadness has softened. Not being a god, my grieving only had the power to mark myself, thankfully, although it did provoke me to *make* marks, to inscribe the effect of this event onto something. My first book of poetry is dedicated to Tara's memory, and several of the poems come from my first attempts to find my way back into language, after the silencing of shock, which felt itself like a kind of unwriting. Unwriting a friendship and its future, unwriting who I was, without her. Unwriting how things might be for her child and her partner, her family, her other friends. Unwriting the texture of daily life. I was new to this feeling, uncomprehending of its intensity, its visceral presence in my gut and my breathing. I was illiterate in the discourse of grief, unlettered in it, and unwilling to learn. But learn I did, because I had no choice.

Sweet Chestnut

Castanea sativa

I am trying to draw the old sweet chestnut again; the one beside the marshy clearing in the wood. I try to draw the suckers springing out from its base above the spongey wet, the moss, grasses and rushes. Willows have grown in the last decade, grass is colonising the boggy parts. The marsh is drying out. My pen snags on the paper. It is a brush pen, the kind you might practise calligraphy with, and the fibres catch and spread as they distribute the ink, dispersing it in a line that is granular, contains gaps.

The tree is solid; I can't get my arms around its girth. I tried once, when I wanted to work out how old it is. I pressed my face and chest to its bark and thought about the way that the tree and I, material bodies in this place together, both have space within us. We both having structures called capillaries in which various fluids are propelled around our bodies. We both have spaces between our atoms and within them.

The tree by the marsh is one of several ancient sweet chestnuts in Bush Wood. They still bear fruit in late summer. In actual fact, they are at most 'veterans' rather than 'ancient', having a trunk girth of at least three metres (veteran) but less than six (ancient). Both veteran and ancient trees show dead wood in their crowns and broken branches, though my veterans don't seem to have the loosened bark or hollowed-out trunks that also mark the last stage of a tree's life.

There is another sweet chestnut close by, on the track that leads from the marsh to the Keeper's Lodge. It has a trunk that forks into a Y, like an arm reaching out. This too is a veteran, marked as such on the Woodland Trust's Ancient Tree Inventory. I see it again, in a black and white postcard amongst a local historian's collection; that distinctively shaped trunk. One hundred and fourteen years after that picture was taken, the tree is still there. The trunk is wider, the crown full of dead wood, but it is the same tree. Those oval, serrated leaves. It has a partner on the other side of the track, opposite the cottage, and there is yet another below the marsh on an overgrown path. If you wield a ruler and a map, you can easily extend a straight line between these two and the veteran chestnut from the postcard. It's likely they once formed part of an avenue; one of the many planted in and around the Wanstead estate in the late seventeenth century by Josiah Child, Governor of the East India Company, Member of Parliament, founder member of the Royal African Company.

Across the junction from where the Lodge stands, there are a pair of stone pillars, carved with the initials – eroded but visible – of Richard Child, Josiah's son, to whom his estate passed at the turn of the eighteenth century. These pillars once held gates to the main entrance to the Wanstead estate. Part of the lock is still embedded in one of them; smoothed iron. The gates were chained shut in the early 1810s by the improbably-named William Pole-Tylney-Long-Wellesley, who upon his marriage to Catherine Tylney-Long not only gained possession of the estate but also two additions to his surname (though the couple went by the less cumbersome Long-Wellesley). The locals were having none of it: the chains were removed, forcibly, by a blacksmith in the employ of a local man and after the subsequent court case, the gates were required to remain open.

Within ten years of the marriage, Long-Wellesley had burned through his wife's inheritance, bankrupted himself and his family and doomed Wanstead House to eventual demolition. Everything – right down to the stone that built this 'definitive work of English Palladianism' – was sold off and dispersed. As Hannah Armstrong reveals in her book about the estate (*Wanstead House: East London's Lost Palace*), little remains that is traceable. A property on Hills Road, Cambridge – also called Wanstead House – contains the great hall's iron banister, some of the marble mantelpieces, wall panelling from two rooms and some cornices. An obelisk from the grounds was moved to Loughton, whilst the first tee at Wanstead Golf Club occupies the site of the house – and the gardens with their ornamental lakes and avenues and follies are now permanently open to the public as Wanstead Park, which would have displeased Long-Wellesley in the extreme.

Most of the trees in those wide avenues were sold for lumber. This was not an unusual fate for an estate's trees – they were usually planted with an eye to their monetary worth – and in fact, Long-Wellesley's son had successfully gained an injunction preventing him doing this before financial ruin, as they represented part of his inheritance. The veteran sweet chestnuts I plotted on my map likely escaped because they were outside the grounds.

Today my walk has ranged further than I expected and I feel tired and morose, stumbling over a loosely tied shoe as I cross Blake Hall Road onto Overton Drive, but the sight of water through a fence and trees draws me on. This road was once the main approach to Wanstead House, curving around an octagonal body of water called The Basin, across which eighteenth-century visitors would have had an impressive view of the Palladian marvel. I think about country estates that I've visited, how I'd stand agog, gaping at double-height libraries and hallways bristling with antlers, imagine myself in the bedroom with the imported Chinese wallpaper, enjoy the vistas outside, the fountains and temples and grottos. The walks and parterres. Fancy myself far from the grit and rush of the city.

But we are never far from the city. Every part of this estate, the remnants of which I glimpse through fencing, is saturated in commerce and exploitation. Even those trees, the survivors I so admire in their arboreal beauty, the remaining avenues so enjoyed by families and walking parties on weekends, were in the end only so much lumber. However they were designed to approximate the sylvan glades of an English pastoral fantasy, they were destined to be cut down once they had achieved maturity and a favourable price. As Raymond Williams showed in *The Country and the City*, his essential study of the literary imagination, the rural and the urban have been entwined for centuries and their relationship structured to favour the men who rule both town and country.

And in the case of Wanstead House, the country isn't even on the same landmass as the city. For after all, Josiah Child made his fortune from both the East India and the Royal African Companies – that is, from colonisation, war and slavery. These are what purchased the services of the garden designers and nurserymen to create such extensive and beautiful grounds, the plants that stocked the family's estate, the lakes and their fish, the grotto with its approximation of the rustic wild. He co-owned 1330 acres of Jamaican land, on which there was a sugar plantation, on which laboured enslaved and indentured people.

These are not the rural workers we are traditionally encouraged to imagine when we think of the pastoral, when we walk the remnants of Picturesque garden design. We are not perhaps meant to think of the people who were forcibly removed from their homes, their families, denied a wage, denied freedom, met with violence, rape, murder. London's commerce made Child rich – small matter to him perhaps that he might be considered with some distaste by his contemporaries as 'nouveau riche' – and made all that violence invisible, turned it into money, houses, pretty landscapes.

That wealth enabled Richard Child to commission a more Picturesque landscaping of the grounds, where you would see a Classical temple, from which you could admire the Palladian front of the house. You'd see a charming grotto, a heronry pond, lakes with islands and be moved, perhaps, to think again of shepherds and pastoral idylls, the beauty of Nature, retreat and solitude. Maybe you'd recite something from Virgil's *Eclogues*, or think of the examples of country house poems you knew. Man (and it is always Man) schools nature to become more harmonious, more beautiful, more Picturesque in this version of English countryside.

But it is a miasma. No matter that Josiah's inheritors divested themselves of those so-called foreign interests eventually. The money was made, inheritance secured. David Dabydeen's 1984 essay pictures the two landscapes as two sides of the same coin; back-to-back, never to face each other (for so whiteness has sought to keep it, the colonised land and its enslaved and indentured workers annexed away from the pleasant grounds and their ornaments, the large house with its many windows). But the coin wears thin, the image stamped comes through. Rising through the artifice of the temple and grotto, the hexagonal Basin, rising through the long slope towards the Ornamental Waters, that other countryside, its inhabitants. It's worth remembering, too, as we enjoy the sight of a rare kingfisher on the lake, the enclosure of common land in this country and the tooling of the law towards the restriction and imprisonment of the poor. Calculations in the name of profit and the enduring contempt of the haves for the have-nots. Those chains around the gate to Wanstead Park.

I pass the length of Wanstead Golf Club's headquarters: red brick wall, a window filled in – and from a glance at the entrance, I notice the building's U shape around a large courtyard and a clock above the central section. This is the estate's former stables, one of the only structures left. And here is a circularity for my circular walk, as I approach the entrance to the park: there are hoof marks on the muddy path, belonging presumably to the horses that are stabled at the riding school in nearby Aldersbrook. It's remarkable to me that there'd be animals like horses kept this far into a city, but it isn't the only example by any means. There is at least one other stables within five miles of where I live – and a couple of miles further into London, there are even two City Farms. *Rus in urbe*; the countryside in town. The rides down which passed the Childs and Tylneys and Long-Wellesleys and their esteemed visitors are now paths and public bridleways, and horses still trot or walk down them, but anyone may learn to ride them now, for a fee.

The stables, grotto and temple are the only structures still standing and in situ; the temple is now a hireable venue for concerts, weddings and other events, and houses a small exhibition about the history of Wanstead Park, whilst the grotto is rather more Picturesque than perhaps first intended, having suffered significant damage in a fire in the late 1880s. The exterior, with its unevenly-sized stones and jagged outline, is very Fake Ruin, familiar from paintings in the Picturesque style – but the inside, what's left of it, is surprisingly orderly. There is a curved channel for water, surrounded by paving and the suggestion of a room in the uniformity of the brick walls that remain. It originally incorporated boat storage and sported walls encrusted with shells, pebbles, and other natural materials. This actual, real ruin of a folly built as an imitation ruin was the second grotto built on the estate. The first, contained within a 'Mount' (a fake hill), was created during Richard Child's ownership and did not survive.

I reach the grotto, heartened by the incandescing of yellow leaves against dark bark, the mallards on the water, the dogwalkers who smile distractedly as they throw a stick, a ball, a chew toy. A golden retriever splashes into the lake, paddles determinedly; brief image of Darcy emerging from the Ornamental Waters, a terrapin attached to his boot, a lager can and a plastic bag adorning him like epaulettes. The owners, who tried to keep the locals out, are gone – and the grounds of their gone estate, artifice of imagined pastoral idyll, were eventually transferred over to the Corporation of London. Where the gentry roamed for their day out in the country, families picnic, people play football, bowls, tennis, golf. They walk, they fly model aircraft, they go jogging. The different pieces of the House have spun off, dispersed, and what is left has gone feral. Condoms and loo paper in the bluebell woods, a smell of piss beside the Grotto, which sprouts all manner of opportunistic plants, including the ubiquitous buddleia. The Park is still a managed landscape, as are the Flats, but the avenues of sweet chestnuts – there is one such leading from the Heronry to the temple, two rows of trees that are surely too young to have been planted in Child's age – are valued for their beauty and their fruit these days, the shade they give, the birds and other creatures they support.

The night of my walk, I have an unsettling dream. I am trying to take apart a chair. If I can disassemble it, the tree from which it was made can reconstitute itself. But I don't have the right tools, and I can't follow the instructions – and the wood is full of holes. Woodworm. I can't touch it. If I touch it, I'll get it. But if I don't touch it, I can't – and anyway, it's too late, I have touched it. I look down at my hands and there is a rough and ashy sore on one finger. I know without looking that the woodworm are boring through my torso, that the ex-tree and I are both infected. There is a sense of panic – and then, a sort of dropping feeling. I pick up the tools again: infected, sure, but there is still the work.

The next day, I visit the sweet chestnut by the marsh again. I imagine its atoms marshalling themselves as I approach. The spaces between my atoms, the spaces between the chestnut's, the atoms themselves when I place my palm on the fissures in its bark; maybe they give each other a tiny whirl for a moment.

Boa Constrictor

Boa constrictor

It is autumn and I'm in Greenwich for the day. I walk in the park under hazy sun, see my first ever goldcrest in a camellia bush, watch the runners labour up the hill to the Observatory. There is a tree at the top where a robin likes to sing, and standing near it, I can look across the river to the top of the Arcelor Mittel Orbit tower in Stratford. That's near home, I tell the robin, which has fallen silent.

Later, I walk towards the station. I'm teaching my class this evening near Waterloo. I could take a riverboat, I think. Much pricier than the Tube, but such a lovely journey. They even serve wine on board. Today I'm living an enchanted, city-dweller's life, the life of someone who can skip around town, dwell in a café, walk in a park, ride a boat if she so wishes, insouciant, unassailed by her To Do list, the need to chase the next contract.

The pavements of Greenwich are crowded – it seems to be always tourist season in Greenwich – so I don't see it at first. Just a man, short-ish, pausing at the entrance to the DLR, his hands up by his shoulders. He looks diffidently at his companions, who've already gone inside and are looking back at him. Then I see what he is holding.

Draped around his neck, it is not a scarf but a snake. Thick-bodied, brown-patchworked, head turning, length undulating – the man holds it at what might be its neck and its tail. People are hurrying by, apparently unaware. I watch between gaps in the foot traffic.

Now a DLR staff member is approaching, warily. Someone passing by says, 'Is he trying to – can he take that on there?'

I don't stay to see the outcome. I head towards the river.

I would say *only in London* – except that I came across a recent report about a man on a bus in Manchester who used a boa constrictor as a face mask. It was wound around his neck and mouth in such a way that one of his fellow passengers on the Swinton to Manchester route thought it was a 'funky mask' –

until it started to unwind itself and move along the handrails. The authorities had a suitably wry response:

> Government guidance clearly states that this [a face covering] needn't be a surgical mask, and that passengers can make their own or wear something suitable, such as a scarf or bandana.

> While there is a small degree of interpretation that can be applied to this, we do not believe it extends to the use of snakeskin - especially when still attached to the snake.

Apart from working assistance animals, creatures abound on the Tube. Large dogs who sprawl across entire aisles at their owners' feet, small dogs in large handbags, cats in baskets – and more rarely, cats out of baskets. I once looked up from my book on a Metropolitan line out to Watford to see an older woman making regal progress down the aisle, wearing a black cat on her shoulders. Its tail was up as it balanced with ease, facing the way they were walking.

And there are other creatures, unintentional passengers: pigeons that board and then are trapped, wasps and flies, bees, craneflies, moths. I watched a painted lady butterfly board at Leytonstone one day in summer and bat itself against the fluorescent tube as we travelled west.

Then there are the less welcome passengers. London's

populations of bedbugs (*Cimex lectularius*) has been increasing in number and spreading quite steadily for some time now: the hotter temperatures of climate change shorten their reproductive cycle, so more of them breed, and DDT, which killed them, has been banned. A 2018 news article explicitly links their spread to the public transport network, where bedbugs have been found on seats in trains and buses. Perhaps it's possible to overdo the marvelling at 'nature' – and marvelling is certainly difficult where parasites are concerned. As Kathleen Jamie asks, 'What are vaccinations for, if not to make a formal disconnection from some of these wondrous other species?'

A boa constrictor appeared on a pavement here in Leytonstone in 2018 – probably an abandoned pet. The photo that accompanies the news report is a strangeness. The snake has been snapped while eating a pigeon: a wing juts out as if the beast is about to take flight, the body is tan and cream and brown, and bent in on itself, distending at the join between feather and scale. A grotesquerie, here on an East London pavement. A shop door is open next to a swinging sign for the local paper and parked cars are nose-to-tail at the kerb. Bystanders have given this composite creature a wide berth – you see a woman's legs opposite the camera's viewpoint. Is this space they've left a reverent space? A disgusted or horrified space? An unnerved space? A marvelling space? A pitying space? It evokes all those reactions in me.

I'm struck, too, by the utter incongruity between the reptile and its surroundings – and how this incongruity renders it so terribly vulnerable. And it's not the only one: a reticulated python (*Malayopython reticulatus*) was found coiled around a boiler in Islington in 2019, and another boa constrictor – yet another abandoned pet – was captured near the river at Barnes in 2020. Momentarily feral snakes, jarringly out of place against concrete and metal. Like the cormorants I saw down on the Thames, darting in between barges and river boats, the muntjac I startled at the side of Bush Road, this creature should not be here; this environment is too unnatural and will surely kill it.

Happily for the Leytonstone boa, the RSPCA capture it and take it to a wildlife centre.

Perhaps it's appropriate that E11 should have its own chimera for a while. The proximity of the High Road to Epping Forest and Wanstead Flats and the rapid transition that's possible from traffic jams and car stereos, pubs and shops and cafés to tracts of grassland and the cool air under deciduous trees seems to open up the possibility of strangeness, where mythical beasts might appear or anything might happen. The metropolis reaches out along the roads and rails, it allows for ingress by these portals and it grabs and swallows – and sometimes what it swallows is uncanny. On the London Underground, Leytonstone is the last stop before the Central Line splits as it forges east. One tine of the fork leads to Epping Forest. Alight at Loughton or Theydon Bois or indeed Epping, the end of the line, and in a few minutes you will have grass and scrub around you, trees nearby and then swiftly overhead.

David Constantine's poem, 'The Forest', is alert to this. It is a June night and his protagonist, drunk, 'on the wrong line', wakes at Leytonstone to see someone, '[n]aked as Adam, with a donkey's head':

> ... Woke again
> Somewhere, I don't know where, the place was dead,
> I heard that wind come down the tunnels, then
> Girl's steps running and the girl who ran
> Got in and sat beside the donkey-man.

The train reaches the city, and the pair alight:

The doors wide open, scents, a hubbub or
Music, a river noise – I knew
It was the forest they were heading for.
My ticket was wrong. I let the damned train start
Back for the city, back to its knotted heart.

The city and its Underground system (our very own labyrinth) are capable of producing their own marvels, but not for Constantine's speaker. Here the train is 'damned', the city's heart is 'knotted', suggestive of tightness and complication. By contrast, at the city's edge, the doors open 'wide' to smells and unfamiliar sounds and water; images of liveliness, expansiveness, a promise of something strange and beautiful held in the forest, something perhaps already familiar. For in this stanza, the line break at 'I knew' enables the line to hold that meaning – that the speaker knows the music, the sound of the river – before it is modulated by the phrase that follows on the next line.

What I find interesting is the way in which the city is necessary to produce this possibility of another life. The Underground gets you there, allowing passage for its residents into and out of the city – and once there, the 'river noise' of that alt-place calls up the city's own rivers and brooks and streams – the Thames of course, and the buried Fleet, East London's Lea and Roding to name but a few – that wind through our snaking, interconnecting streets to join each other, to pass beyond the urban edge. Both the Underground and the rivers partake of the city and not-city, joining each to each, holding the flavour of both, ferrying inhabitants between the two. The forest, realm of magic and transformation – as it is for Bottom in *A Midsummer Night's Dream*, which surely Constantine is referencing here – is accessible. You only need Tube fare.

The forest doesn't always offer beauty or benevolent magic – and it isn't always the pastoral or transformative retreat from the city I have been imagining. People have been murdered there or take their own lives or find themselves camping out there, having lost their homes. There is a homeless person in Constantine's poem, a stereotype the speaker compares himself to ('some forgotten dosser in a pew'), in order to contrast the 'well of happiness' the couple create, the donkey-man's dignity, the beauty of the fields and woods to which they travel with his own, urbanised, ordinarily human status. Before the pandemic, a morning walk in Bush Wood would often take me past tents pitched in the many small clearings. The owners would get moved on or encouraged into temporary accommodation periodically. I think about the homeless man I talked with briefly at Kings Cross station once. One of the worse things, he said, about homelessness, and having to beg, was the way people didn't look at him when he spoke to them. The other was 'the vermin. Lice, scabies, bedbugs...'

Ring-necked Parakeet
Psittacula krameri

An evening walk. The light is gold, falling to pink in the west as the sun sets, and a long line of Canadas pass overhead, flying north-east. The moon above Bush Wood is large and full, already visible in the clear sky. There is water in the craters at its poles – and NASA have announced today that they've detected water on its sunlit surfaces as well.

A riot of squawking starts up from the London planes that edge the green space. This is the main reason I come down here. For suddenly, on a signal indecipherable to humans, they set off; a large flock of parakeets – twenty? thirty? – flying low and fast over the grass, heading south-west. More squawking from the eastern edge of the field, a couple of individuals fuss between trees

– and then again, at least thirty of them, eye level with me, noisy, speeding. A mother and son pause to watch the green birds with their fine, long tails and raise their mobile phones to capture the sight. She sees me watching; we smile.

It feels a bit like kinship here on the Flats. The clear sky and the people below it; joggers and families, couples, prams, dogs, the grass and the trees and the Avenue, these sharp-winged birds; all of us beneath the moon and her water. Another huge flock heads west and I duck as they pass, a scant foot it seems, above and around me – for I feel the air vibrate with their wing beats.

Where did the London parakeets come from? It is unlikely that they are descended from any that Jimi Hendrix released on Carnaby Street in the sixties – and nor are they descended from escapees from the set of *The African Queen*. Similarly, the Great Storm of 1987 did not damage any aviary at Syon House – although two butterflies did escape from the London Butterfly House after their lepidopterarium was broken by a fallen tree.

These theories are all great stories – and if you live in

London, you will probably have heard at least one – but they are not true, as a 2020 paper published in the *Journal of Zoology* has reluctantly concluded, after extensive research using both geographical profiling and the British Newspaper Archive. The paper suggests instead that breeding populations of parakeets became established in the 1960s as the result of intermittent and unconnected small-scale releases of privately-owned pets – and notes, drily, that *Psittacula krameri* 'has not needed the help of either rock stars or movie stars to become established.'

Even if the legend of Jimi Hendrix isn't true, Heald et al do demonstrate how well- and long-established the ring-necked (or rose-ringed) parakeet is in the UK. The first newspaper report of parakeets at large in Britain dates from 1855 – they were recorded in Norfolk – and a breeding pair raised five chicks in Lincoln's Inn Fields in 1886. They appear in Loughton cemetery and Epping Forest in an Essex newspaper report in 1932. By the mid-1980s, parakeets number at least five hundred in the wild, with Esher Rugby Club a well-known location for birdwatchers to see them.

Ring-necked parakeets originate from the Indian subcontinent and south of the Sahara in Africa. The London ring-necked parakeets are thought to be from two of the Indian subspecies. They travel far from where they roost at night, to nest and to feed. They feed on arable crops – a threat to farming, there, though the London Bird Atlas minimises this as 'currently localised and not commonplace' – as well as a range of native and non-native trees: for example, horse chestnut buds, sweet chestnuts and fruit trees, and a range of fruits or seeds from other trees, including the London plane. They also visit garden birdfeeders. They are found in all parts of London and have spread as far as Devon and Aberdeenshire. They are classed as an Invasive Alien Species, and there have been reports that culling has been considered by DEFRA.

Native. Non-native. Invasive. Alien. Migrant. These words from the lexicons of ornithology and botany take on a certain, unwelcome resonance that is all the more pressing at the time of writing. Jini Reddy bumps up against such terms in *Wanderland*, an account of her search for the spiritual amongst the flora of the British Isles. She makes the connection:

> I have always felt uncomfortable with the whole "native" and "non-native" trees talk. If you were to replace the word "tree" with people it would all start to sound ominous.

For her, these connotations cannot be eradicated. The vocabulary of science may well occur in a context of intended objectivity, but the slippage between trees and people is already there in the language from which it derives: 'A non-native tree is a foreigner tree, an outlier, an interloper. I know the mantra – I've heard it intoned often enough.'

Whatever their origins, the birds that call to each other as they edge along the upper branches of the oaks and chestnuts in the wood have only ever known the British Isles. Their species is 'established', has a 'breeding population'; at what point is a species deemed 'native'? Or will that never happen? Perhaps parakeets will be deemed an 'introduced' species at some point, as the sweet chestnut is? Or, eventually, an 'ancient introduction', like the osier? I appreciate the usefulness of such terms as shorthand for the history of a plant or an animal's relationship with its environment, but as Mark Fountain says, 'words matter':

> ... especially when they come from those in power. To brand parakeets invaders is to fundamentally misrepresent their nature and ignore the role humans have played in their story.

For, as Fountain points out, 'We move plants and animals around the world with the casualness of rearranging furniture.' In his essay, written for the website of Flock Together, a birdwatching collective for People of Colour, he articulates the way in which this import and export of living beings is inextricable from the legacy of Empire.

Alien. Invasive. Non-native. For Fountain, as for Reddy with her trees, the parallels between the language used to describe the rose-ringed parakeet and British people like himself who find themselves racialised are painfully clear. After all, 'nature' is a concept devised by humans – and scientific discourses are as enmeshed in the languages and cultures that produced them as anything else. Fountain makes a strong argument for change – and with habitats and migratory patterns themselves changing as a result of human action and consequent climate change, this could be the moment. What would a new vocabulary, fit for the meticulous attention of ornithologists and shorn of its colonial overtones, look like? What words could do justice to the history of those birds speeding low over the grass?

Lesser Redpoll

Carduelis cabaret

My face lifted up to the white sky. Flecks pepper my cheeks. Yes, like ground black pepper, they itch a little. I sight drifting, floating; a stream of particles falling diagonally from the tree in front of me.

My face lifted up to the delicate: seedheads, shine and pallor of silver birch bark, the branches in silhouette – and amongst them, small tails, brisk movement. Silently at work, redpoll, a small flock.

I watch the tiny birds, industrious and swift feeders. I can't quite see their markings. The London Birders have reported sightings of redpoll and linnets on the Heath in recent days, but I'm not confident and nor is my eyesight. They are so very small, though – and I catch sight of a streaky breast, enough to name them.

They are intent upon feeding, hanging upside down from the smallest outgrowths of the tree; twigs and stems that bend a little under their weight. They move amongst each other; it is so quiet this early weekend morning that I think I can hear their beaks cracking the seed hulls. I squat down to the grass to look at the debris from their feeding, the scattered flecks of husk.

Lesser redpoll used to be abundant all over Britain until the seventies. Now they're on the 'red list', meaning that their species is threatened with extinction. These birds are likely to be winter visitors; their territory has shifted north and east and their population has fast declined. I brush the bits from my face and walk off through the broom and dead grass to cross the road and head back through Bush Wood. I am barely beneath the trees when *pip-pipping* blooms out all around me. Again, I catch sight of tails – long ones, this time. Long-tailed tits: I often see them here. Their call sounds more deliberate than the other titmice and I love their sporty black stripe, fawn-coloured breast, the tails like rudders. I see them in the garden too, in mixed flocks with great tits and blue tits, moving companionably from tree to shrub to birdfeeder. I smile, thinking of the birds' obliviousness to human affairs. I have come out here yet again to walk off the feeling that something awful is going to happen and we're all going to die. What do the birds care? They don't feel dread, they just get on with living while they can. And look, Meryl: for this moment, here in this place, redpoll are feeding in numbers. We aren't quite at the end, yet. Nothing is certain.

Swallow

Hirundo rustica

WHERE THE PLACE?
UPON THE HEATH.
THERE TO MEET WITH

It is March. I am in a bad mood and I can't write, so I go for a walk. I am having trouble with a Difficult Person and don't know what to do. I head out to the Heath, with a vague notion to check the witches' tree I discovered the other week. I want to see if they have replenished the ribbons. Maybe I'll meet one of them.

It is cold and I stomp the sodden track at speed. Tara's birthday was the other day – another one she's missed – and I've only just realised. Not even ten years she's been gone. The wind knocks into me and I take a great gulp of air. The houses always look as if they have drawn back out here, as if the city has opened its hand wide to the sky. There is an open feeling that not even the crawling lines of traffic and the stink of exhaust fumes can dispel. I look at the trees that border the open space. Where their crowns taper and widen, where the branches end – where there is sky – that is where I locate the Open, a place that is part tree, part air.

Is this what death is like? The Open? It might not be so terrible to be transformed into something like that, into tree and air. No self or consciousness, but still part of the world, its particles.

How is a moor different from a heath? How is a heath different from a blasted heath? A moor is found in highland and experiences high rainfall. A heath is found in lowland and is connected with humans and their actions. The soil is less fertile and drains readily, growing bracken and gorse as well as heather. With the increasing amount of nitrogen in the atmosphere, due in no small part to the use of fertilizers in crop farming, heathland is in danger of disappearing – and the plants and creatures that live there too – as its soil becomes more fertile, less supportive to its specialized residents. Human-produced nitrogen has increased by five times in the last fifty years. Maybe the witches will meet in a wood or scrubland next time.

How is a heath different from a blasted heath? Maybe it isn't. Maybe a heath is customarily blasted; open land for wind and rain to race over. And Wanstead Heath was blasted by wildfires too, last summer – so, on this March day, it looks particularly bereft. Hawthorns stand blackened and budless. One oak has a scorch mark up its trunk. Some of the broom has regenerated quickly since the fires, but the new clumps are substantially shorter than other, more established growth further south. It is still a living heath, I think, looking at the resilient broom, a very low eruption that might be gorse – as if nature is there to provide me with 'inspiration', to furnish me with metaphors that might induce hope, to help me believe the lie that 'life finds a way', that 'Nature' (female personified of course) will always revive and prevail. If life does indeed find a way, then humans are fast shutting it down.

I pass another dead tree, jump across a iced-over puddle and skid on the surrounding mud, cursing. If I didn't feel so wretched, it would be hilarious, this grumpy, short person windmilling her arms to keep her balance. I feel ridiculous and embarrassed as well as angry, now. And sad.

Whenever I visit my mother
I feel I am turning into Emily Bronte,
my lonely life around me like a moor,
my ungainly body stomping over the mud flats with a look of
        transformation
that dies when I come in the kitchen door.

This is part of the third stanza of 'SHE', a section from the beginning of Anne Carson's long poem, 'The Glass Essay'. It comes to mind as I finish my grumpy walk. I don't know what I'm turning into, but these lines speak to me. Something to do with the twinning of 'ungainly' with 'stomping' reminds me of my skid-and-flail through the mud. It's even evoked by the arrangement on the page: the transition of that long fourth line – taking flight as an imagination might take flight, expanding as one's sense of self might expand among plants and creatures, temporarily relieved of the social – to the fifth, which so emphatically reels the utterance back in to land glumly on those two sour and unpromising monosyllables at the start. And there's something about the life being likened to a moor, the self so marooned and exposed, that sums up my lost, ruffled state.

Where the ground goes down into a depression,
  the ice has begun to unclench.
Black open water comes
  curdling up like anger […]

Out on my Heath, anger and transformation and the giant, cold puddles the crows like to bathe in are everywhere this March. It has rained and rained – and then it has frozen. If I move over the puddles quickly enough, I only crack the surface of the ice; the nearest I'll ever get to walking on water. The crows keep up a racket. The trees have been truly blasted – by fire and now fierce rain and hail, this ice. Their bareness is darkened by char and smoke amongst their unburnt and living neighbours.

And now it is April. I walk the Heath again – our shared municipal Heath – and admire the way the arms of the trees are flung open to the sky, some with buds like studs or bolts along a piece of iron, waiting to burst more juicily, for sap to flow. Some of them already have tiny green or pink ruffles at their tips, but all – except the burnt ones – are beginning; sap coming faster, adjusting to the longer days, our planet's tilt, the incoming new season.

From behind my head, erratic flitter, zipping north, as if popped from a cyst, as if burst from bud; a swallow. Yes, a veritable swallow shoots from behind me, like an unevenly fletched arrow, jittery and veering in its flight. It's so fast that it's gone almost as soon as I register the shape, the extreme pointiness of the wings, suggestion of forked tail.

In *The Natural History of Selbourne*, the naturalist Gilbert White devotes much consideration to the question of where swallows go in winter. He can't quite jettison his belief – a common one during the eighteenth century – that swallows hibernated under the ground, or under bodies of water in *hibernaculum*, which could be translated from the Latin as a 'tent for winter quarters', but seems to have been imagined as small caverns or tunnels, or the muddy bottom of rivers and other bodies of water or iced-over bogs. When I try to imagine this, I see bubbles under the water, or bubbles in the water resting on the pond floor, or bubbles within the mud and silt; I see a half-watery, half-earthy medium from which the bird streaks, breaking surface in Spring.

'Are not these late hatchlings more in favour of hiding than migration?' he asks, in a letter to Thomas Pennant. Over and over in his *Natural History*, he returns to the question, unable to countenance their migration to and from southern Africa. And White's not the only one. His contemporary, John Hunter, the eminent founder of 'scientific surgery', was so exercised by the disappearance of swallows at summer's end that he conducted an experiment, keen to prove one or other of the differing theories then in circulation. As autumn approached, twenty birds were trapped in a specially-built room, containing such items as suspended pipes, cave-like holes and a water tub filled with reeds and other materials. All but one died.

They starved, no doubt. Or froze. Here is an image of a small swift bird, dashing itself less and less swiftly as it tires and starves, against stone walls, against its siblings, perching wearily on a pipe or the edge of a tub, shunting up against the others in the dark for warmth, falling stunned or exhausted to the floor. A sole survivor streaking out the door towards the air and light, towards food, towards – pulled by – its other home.

This other home was the one that Gilbert White was unwilling to entertain. As Anne Mellor observes, the 'swallow represented all that was best in English country life' for him, the emblem of 'an idealised English national identity'. Furthermore, he could not believe that such tiny creatures had the strength to travel so far. And what was Africa to White? Perhaps a far-off clime that had nothing to do with him, tucked away in Selborne. Yet White's century is a century of slavery – the same century in which the inheritors of Wanstead House squander the fortune made in no small part from the trade in human beings. It is the century of Ignatius Sancho, of Olaudah Equiano's memoir of enslavement; it is the century which saw the continuation of a strong African presence in London, famous and not so famous, enslaved as well as free. It is the century of Ottobah Cugoano and the Sons of Africa, the century in which London rose to dominance as a trading centre for slavery. And it is the century in which White's nephew, Dr John White, who spent much of his childhood in Selbourne, acquired shares in a plantation in Montserrat and its 'stock'.

ALL: FAIR IS FOUL, AND FOUL IS FAIR:
 HOVER THROUGH THE FOG AND FILTHY AIR.

[WITCHES VANISH]

The Vernal Equinox is well over; the days start earlier, the evening light goes slowly. I pass again the hawthorn tree, adorned with black lace garter and wisps of shiny ribbon. The branches to which they're tied are dead, but the tree has put out new growth, closer to its core, so that it is a column of green with its own radial spokes. I wonder if the witches will venture out here to their tree again, come May Day.

BANQUO: The earth hath bubbles, as the water has,
                   And these are of them: whither are they vanished?
MACBETH: Into the air, and what seemed corporal, melted,
                   As breath into the wind.

Macbeth and Banquo, returning from battle, are as confounded by the witches' origin as the eighteenth century is about its swallows – and as full of conjecture. The women spring into view, they disappear: whither *are* they vanished? The practical answer is, of course, through the trapdoor in the Elizabethan stage. But in the world the play creates, I imagine the witches having bubble-homes just as the swallows did, environments that are neither one thing nor another: blisters, cysts, the heath's unnatural growth of a membrane of sorts that splits to admit the three aberrant creatures (they have beards, they are without men) and seals itself behind them. The other interpretation – found in the second edition of the Arden Shakespeare – is that Banquo is just comparing the witches to bubbles. Pop – they're gone!

The witches tell each other stories and make plans together, they speak in rhythms and rhymes that sound like children's songs. In place of prophecy, they offer Macbeth riddles, conjuring visions out of their bubble-like cauldron, which he misunderstands. They were never intended as such, but the witches have become my touchstone, with their sisterhood and their withered wildness, the way they bring into being possible worlds, as difficult to translate as birdsong. Some interpretations of the play suggest it is as if the land itself gives voice.

Out on Wanstead Flats, out in the open and alone, I whisper, I mutter, I growl. I wheeze and rasp. Hover in the fog and filthy air. The heath is bounded on all sides by roads, often busy, and the traffic noise obscures my voice. The crows kick up a racket with their own rasping voices.

STAY YOU IMPERFECT SPEAKERS

Burnt hawthorns put out their shoots. Oaks with broken crowns and limbs cracked off by the storms are in early leaf. The boughs rest on the mud, the icy puddles, their shoots angling away and up towards the light. Stumps and bare, charred wood and buds on the same tree. I haven't seen another swallow out here since that first startlement, though I know that housemartins swoop low over their own reflections in nearby Wanstead Park and the swifts will soon return (though nothing like the great train of ten or more that used to steam across the sky above our house). I haven't seen any likely witches, either, although how would I know? I yomp around the Flats and speculate about Gilbert White's swallows and Macbeth's witches and Swedish ice ponds and eighteenth-century *hibernaculum* and Elizabethan miasmic bubbles. Just beyond the corner of my vision, Anne Carson's speaker stalks her moor, cut off from her lover but surviving somehow, troubled by her difficult relationship with her mother but in relationship nonetheless: 'my ungainly body stomping over the mudflats with a look of transformation'. A swallow crosses the acid grassland, bordered by three roads. The witches tie ribbons to their tree, presiding over a place that is all paradox – dead and alive, solid and immaterial – and holds something other, something alt. Change is possible here. It is always possible in the feral borough.

WHERE THE PLACE
UPON THE HEATH
THERE TO MEET WITH

Jersey Tiger Moth

Euplagia quadripunctaria

Like an oversized plectrum left on the windowsill. Like a twist of paper or crisp packet corner, but with volition. A long triangle, striped and firm of outline, with inner flashes of red, effecting an angled spiral towards street tree, then flat against the fissures in *Tilia x europaea's* bark.

Territory ever outwards, ever northwards. North warmer. North wetter. O grazer of nettle and bramble, deigning to suburbs now; the first time I saw you, I was standing to stretch by a window, my eyes full of screen and words. One of my hands reflected, marked by stripes, then my thumb detaching itself, zig-zagging away from the glass, describing circles downwards. Ten years or so, and you're a Londoner, *Euplagia quadripunctaria*: jazzy looker, summer flitter.

White-flowered Honesty

Lunaria annua var. *albiflora*

A few fine days after a spell of dull weather. There is a giddiness. The air is scented with barbecues and most of our neighbours are in their gardens every day with friends, family, wine, burnt meat. My beloved and I are both working on writing projects and skulk inside, content to enjoy the view. Nubs of rhubarb appear in the garden; the black kale I abandoned (cavolo nero, *Brassica olerocea*) bursts into flower. More blooms: wallflowers (*Erysimum cheiri*) and greater periwinkle (*Vinca major*) on our front wall – and out on the Flats, a riot. Blackthorn froth everywhere, alexanders – I'd never noticed alexanders before, thought they were a seaside plant – and gorse. Then broom, hawthorn, bluebells.

I find patches of grape hyacinth, rogue daffodils; garden

escapees. Beside the alexanders, which I'm so delighted to have noticed and to have identified, there is another plant, which I think at first is garlic mustard. It has the same four petals to its white flowers, and the leaves come to a point from a broadly triangular base, with an uneven, 'toothed' edge. But looking more closely, I see the flowers are bigger, and the leaves are heart-shaped, with sharper teeth than garlic mustard. It takes a conversation with a passing plant lover on social media to identify it as a garden dweller, white-flowered honesty, that has somehow wandered to this grass-and-nettle verge where the track meets the road.

Out in real life, I am not doing much conversation. My own wandering has become moody; I am fed up with sharing my walks with my fellow residents. When people went to offices to work and gyms to work out, these tracks were much quieter. I chide myself for resenting the appearance of dog walkers, joggers, couples, families as they surprise me out of my introspection. It is a privilege to only have this to resent, sharing these green spaces with other people.

If I could be invisible, I would. If I could silence the talkers or momentarily stop up my ears, I would. If I could take flight into the arms of that tree or perch on the top of the mobile phone mast by Centre Road like our local Egyptian geese, I would. For in those moments of 'no', I am fully in the quiet alongside the plants and creatures around me, attending to the feeling of the ground through my soles and the slight friction of my clothing as I walk. And in those moments, pausing in the cool to stare up into a horse chestnut's canopy, tracking the scritch of grey squirrel claws, something happens. It is as if the wood and its inhabitants combine to make Another; some larger being that takes in one breath and turns to look at me. Or as if it notices what's happening in the wood and enters.

What is it? This something that flickers into view at times of extremity, when both my senses and emotions are intensified, or when I am alone and feel free enough to range the plains and halls of thought. This something else, more, made, each moment, by my attention.

Whatever it is, I have often felt it nearest here, in the feral borough that rises up around us as we go about our daily lives; the herb robert in the crack between wall and pavement, the shepherd's purse at the foot of the CPZ sign, the river threading through from east to west, the gulls and cormorants attending it. It's here in the cocked head of a feral pigeon, eyeing up my park bench sandwich, the way the London planes rustle and crackle in the wind. Sun falls on the worn grass of a city square, a great tit *pinks* from a cherry laurel. Blackbirds as dusk comes on, a spider splayed on a warm brick wall.

Six-toed Cat

Felis catus x. polydactyl

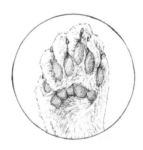

A summer afternoon. I shift my grip on the Bag for Life and continue walking past the empty opticians, the ex-beauty salon. A large white-and-black cat detaches itself from shadow, pads across the grass towards me in a manner I can only describe as regal, pauses with tail arched high, deigns to receive my greeting.

An older woman with a shopping trolley pauses, smiles. 'I used to have a cat like that,' she says. 'Black and white.'

We both agree the cat is lovely. She's about to move on when something catches her eye. She frowns.

'Oh no. There's something wrong with it. Should we –' she looks around. 'Its feet.'

I squat down by the creature, which enthusiastically rubs

the side of its head against my hand, purring. I see what the woman has noticed.

'It's all right. It's just one of those cats with six toes.'

She looks unconvinced.

'I read about it.'

I don't tell her the next thoughts that bounce into my head but they are there, warming up on my tongue, anxious for lift-off.

My dad had six toes on his left foot. The extra one caused him no end of nuisance. He had wide feet as well and my childhood involved a lot of listening to monologues about his running shoes; which brand gave his feet most room, which would give him bruised toenails.

The other thought I do not share is that Ernest Hemingway's house in Key West, Florida, is populated by six-toed cats – about sixty, according to the website – some of which are descendants of his original pet, Snow White, reputedly given to him by a ship's captain. For years I harboured a desire to visit Ernest Hemingway's house in order to see the cats. The writer and his prose style, his drinking, his masculinity – not so interested. But six-toed cats, I thought, that would be a wonder. They are sometimes called Hemingway cats, although they are more properly called polydactyl cats.

I think of Dad and his six toes every so often with a little shock. It is a remarkable thing that no one will see, now he's gone. So here it is; my dad had six toes on his left foot. He was born in one of the bombing raids on London in 1940. His mother and the doctors chose not to cut off the extra toe. The first time he tasted ice cream, he was five, and he asked if they could heat it up. There are a multitude of facts like this, little things about him that no one will ever know, unless I tell them.

The woman says goodbye and I raise my hand to stroke the six-toed cat again, but it has already spotted someone on the low fence nearby with a sandwich and is off to make a new friend. Extra, excess, because matter likes to repeat its forms. I'm not Christian, but it's stuck in my mind, something the former Archbishop of Canterbury, Rowan Williams, said in an interview once:

> God's act in creating the world is gratuitous, so everything comes to me as a gift. God simply wills that there shall be joy for something other than himself.

Common Wood Pigeon, again
Columba palumbus

It is another blistering day in Leytonstone and I'm trying to work in the back room. A large aeroplane passes rowdily overhead and I hear raised voices from across the gardens. We all have our windows open, trying to make the most of the faint breeze. The house is porous to noise; it feels companionable. There is the sound of a bird's heavy landing in a tree; much wing-ruffling, leaf-shaking and then that distinctive call. Wood pigeons. The neighbour's plum has set fruit this year and the plump, grey birds feast and call upon its balconies and ledges.

Later, I shut all the windows and curtains in the house against the heat – the air grips my body when I throw some cartons into the recycling bin – and huff on my inhaler, sparing a thought for the people who have no choice but to pack onto the Tube, endure badly-ventilated workplaces. During this week, I know the outside only by its sounds: aeroplanes on their flight paths, labouring over their figure-eights and descents, the odd car, the postie's *beep* as he scans a package. Swifts screaming, blue tits chittering.

One of the birds starts to purr; familiar and sleepy-sounding in the heat.

I listen harder.

two TWO two two two

two TWO two two two

There are more parts to the wood pigeon's call than I thought, and the more I listen, the more the syllables morph until I cannot hear, any more, *two two* or *fool* or *fail* or *you*. I just hear a bird in a tree, calling for a mate, warning off its rivals. I think about Dad's last year, sitting with him and Mum outside their flat, enjoying the swifts speeding through the sky's clear blaze and the wood pigeon calling from the weeping willow.

I am over halfway through my life and it seems suddenly wrong, now, in this shady room with my books and our furniture around me, my good fortune and relative health, not to appreciate every single thing about this life I have. Success and failure. Performing and hiding. Civilised and uncivilised. They go on and on, these unhelpful binaries by which I've lived my life and in this I am not unique. In none of this am I unique, but I only have one of me. It's time to stop trying to corral everything into these categories. I can obey the inimical thoughts, I can wash my hands as many times as I like, but it won't keep away the bad feelings. Sadness, fear, anger, grief; they're all part of it, just as much as happiness or contentment.

A concrete bench and the smell of pine. A small bird with a long, bobbing tail. A string of sharp-winged visitors, veering across the sky for a few weeks, and then gone. I want to live my life fully, companionable with my fellow creatures. That one in the tree outside now; so plump it seems furry, purring to itself in between calls like a cat.

The bird's voice fades. A clatter of wings and it's off.

Wren

Troglodytes troglodytes

So here I am again, out in my wood, which is not mine at all but – being officially part of Epping Forest – the City of London's, which is to say, everyone's. I am walking slowly this time. It is lunchtime in autumn. I have more regular work this year – still teaching, still running poetry workshops – and must take my exercise between classes and meetings. I edge around mud patches and hold back bramble strands until I reach a clearing, full of grey poplar saplings. Sunshine. I have been listening to great tits and blue tits, robins, wood pigeons, crows, a gull – and now a parakeet starts up, raucous above my head. I turn right, plunge back into shade, picking my way between the brackish puddles that occupy most of the track.

Then, piercing, sweet, shockingly loud: a wren. I stop to listen properly.

I think about the different ways of naming; of the common names and what they show me, the scientific names and how they were conceived. How does calling a plant by its common name affect me differently to calling it by its botanical name? Why, for example do I love to call the wren *Troglodytes troglodytes*, when it announces itself from a hedge or thicket? Such a long name in Greek for such a small bird, such an announcing name with those hard consonant sounds, the consonance of *t* and *d* sounds. And such a small common name; the light lift of the *r* sound into the monosyllable, the light landing of the *n* sound at the end. And yet, the wren is LOUD. Who would've thought that such a tiny bird would have such a big voice? Maybe a double-barrelled, polysyllabic name is appropriate, hovering above or under the name we know in the English language. Maybe, actually, I need the bird to have both – a giant name for its giant song, a tiny word for its tiny self.

We have the word 'wren' from the Old English 'wrenna'. The Latin name came about because it was thought that wrens lived in caves. The bird's name in German, *Zaunkönig*, means 'king of the fence/hedge' and in Dutch, it means 'king of winter' (*winterkoning*). In Britain, we have *Jenny Wren*, often partnered with Robin Redbreast in nursery rhymes. Her earliest appearance in print dates from the late seventeenth century, though *Jenny* has been used as a prefix to denote a female animal since at least 1600. Confusingly, the plant we call herb robert in Britain (*Geranium robertianum*), is called 'Jenny Wren' in the United States.

Meanwhile, the wren emits another blast from the holly behind me; this tiny, round bird with the bars on its wings and its short, abruptly upright tail, unaware of, indifferent to the names we give it.

There must be ways of knowing a thing for its own sake, without its name – of being with a plant or a bird, an animal or insect, without succumbing to the urge to identify. It is possible to acknowledge without taxonomy the wood pigeon's flight of arc and wing-clap and glide, for example. The pleasure I feel watching the way poplar leaves move in the wind, revealing their paler undersides; does it matter or not that I know what those trees are called? That I can tell whether it is osier or goat willow here by the dried-up pond-become-marsh? Maybe if I resisted the urge to name, it would enable me to be more with the world, to just be with it, rather than always wanting something from it.

Still, knowing the names of those willows would matter if I were studying the effects of pollutants upon urban plantlife, or tracking the changes wrought by climate change upon the green spaces of London – and I'd benefit too from all the different, meticulous knowledge frameworks built up by generations of scientists before me. It matters to me that other humans found out how to eat the plant, to use the good of it to ease pain or illness, to husband it by coppicing and use its pliant wood to make useful things. Not only do I have access to aspirin and a very capacious laundry basket because of the people before me, but learning about this brings me into relationship with them as well as with the plant, enriching the way I relate to the world around me.

I move on a few steps along the track, hoping that my absence will encourage the wren to sing again, and look up into the crowns of the oaks with their scant, yellowing leaves. A wood pigeon launches itself above them, clapping wings, holding them out and steady, gliding in a deep arc. So exuberant a display it seems, with such energy; it can't just be the pairing and mating imperative that makes the bird do that, I think. But what a human thought. Who knows if pigeons feel joy?

This is the philosophical question that Thomas Nagel addresses in his paper, 'What is it Like to Be a Bat?' He argues that even if we could change from human into bat, we could never accurately imagine our bat experiences beforehand – and nor could we, as bats, compare them to our human experiences. Our mind's 'present constitution' (bat-mind, human-mind) prevents us. Nagel's thesis uncovers, by extension, the folly of believing that we can ever achieve total objectivity in our thinking. We will never completely become the impartial observer, accurately perceiving and understanding the objects of our attention. If we always think of them as just that, objects, with all the other-ing and thing-ing implicit in the word, we miss crucial parts of the picture: not just our own subjectivity, but our relationship with what we are looking at, the way in which we affect them and they affect us even if we never actively interact.

Materialism – the concept that only matter and its actions exist in the universe, nothing else – will always set us up as subject and object, self and other, either side of an unbridgeable divide. That way of thinking can never accurately understand and represent subjectivity. Maybe we are better off focusing on what happens in that gap instead – or trying to think of other ways in which our consciousness can be in and with the world. The French philosopher Maurice Merleau-Ponty, and the branch of philosophy called phenomenology, have offered a way of thinking that emphasises a relationship, rather than a divide. In his

Phenomenology of Perception, Merleau-Ponty presents perception as a kind of reciprocity between the self and the world, challenging the subject-object, outside-inside divisions of materialism. When we perceive, he says, 'we situate ourselves in ourselves and in the things, in ourselves and in the other, at the point where, by a sort of chiasm, we become the others and we become world.' This 'chiasm' is what phenomenology offers us instead of the 'gap'; an exchange:

> The chiasm is not only a me other exchange (the messages he receives reach me, the messages I receive reach him), it is also an exchange between me and the world, between the phenomenal body and the 'objective' body, between the perceiving and the perceived: what begins as a thing ends as consciousness of the thing, what begins as a 'state of consciousness' ends as a thing.

I am joined to this world in which I move, to which I respond – by my senses and the way I understand the information they give me. My dual experience as perceiver and perceived is simultaneous, so that I am, in a strange way, both 'inside' (in my body-self) and 'outside' (perceiving beyond my body's material boundary). Perception conditions our relationship with the world so totally that to try and think of self and world as somehow existing objectively for us outside our perceptions is pointless.

All this might seem far away from Tiny-but-Mighty-Troglodytes-Troglodytes, who is still singing in that bush and being answered by another somewhere in front of and above me. But between and below, beside and adjacent to their song trails, I am standing here as the scent of my own sweat and deodorant, my shampoo and the fabric detergent with which I washed my clothes disperses into the air we share. My body heat too, and the space I occupy, the weight I press into the mud, the sound of my breathing and my half-voiced exclamation when the second wren begins to sing; I sense it all, it is all sensed.

For I can't know what they make of me, the wrens. Are they aware of me? Large-Possible-Trampler-Killer. Stinker-Giant. Noisy-Monster. I can name myself for them as much as I want but it will never bridge the gap set up by the materialist's subject-object relationship. I will never know myself from outside myself. I will never know the world from outside myself. And I will never know the world as a wren.

Can I try again? There is singing, the sound is in me and the air just as my breath is in me and the air. I am not the singer but I am with the singer.

And then I walk on.

Yarrow

Achillea millefolium

The first part of yarrow's botanical name is there because of Achilles, who – the story goes – learnt its uses in childhood from Chiron, wisest of centaurs. In Homer's *Iliad*, Achilles' boyhood friend Patroclus uses it to heal the Thessalian king, Eurypylus, wounded in battle:

> With warm water
> he washed the black blood flowing from the wound,
> then rubbed between his hands into a powder
> over the wound a bitter yarrow root,
> that dulled all pangs of pain. Now the gash dried
> as the blood and powder clotted.

Chiron, master of healing arts, whose name comes from the

word for 'hand' in Ancient Greek, who became the constellation Centaurus, haunts yarrow's name, a silent prefix perhaps.

The second half of the name – *millefolium* – refers to the leaves' shape; each frond seems to be made of many little leaves, fern-like to my eyes. And its common names mostly attest to either those multi-part leaves or its usefulness in healing wounds; hundred-leaved grass, lace plant, milfoil, nosebleed, nose pepper, old man's pepper, sanguinary, savory tea, soldier's woundwort, thousand-leaf, thousand-seal, thousand weed. It encourages scar tissue to form – presumably, why it was so useful to the *Iliad*'s battle-wounded soldiers – and can help reduce muscle spasms. It is also reputed to be an emmenagogic – that is, it 'restores the menstrual flow' – and a tea can be made from the leaves to relieve cold symptoms; with the addition of cayenne pepper, it 'will cause profuse perspiration and thus speed recovery.' I laugh when I read this. I need no help in perspiring.

I find it first by the gate that bars the track to the Keeper's Lodge at the corner of Bush Road and Blake Hall Road. The white, umbelliferous flowerheads are tightly packed with petals; the leaves are pretty and feathery. I am bleeding when I come across it; a surprise in both ways. My periods have been intermittent for a year or so now; sparse and spotting when they come, barely worth a tampon.

Later, I notice the plant amongst the grasses at the edge of the playing field, and as the summer progresses without the customary football matches and training sessions – it is a pandemic year, there are still restrictions – on the unmown pitches themselves. Unkempt and straggly, the pitches grow out their white markings, collect gulls beside their puddles, proliferate their weeds: dandelion, redshank, greater plantain, ribwort plantain, red dead-nettle, black horehound. Rings of fungi appear. I enjoy tracking their progress, spotting more vegetal incursions into the sportsground.

On one walk, I encounter a mother and her daughters collecting flower heads. When I ask the teenager what they are doing, she shrugs, embarrassed, the yarrow cupped loosely in a hand. Or maybe she thinks I am about to have a go at them for picking wildflowers. I want to ask them if they'll make a tea, or how you might heal a wound with yarrow, or if they use it as a flavouring or in home-made beauty treatments, but instead I smile at the teenager in an encouraging way and pass on.

A few months before he got really frail, my dad came to hear me at a poetry event. It was the first time I had read from my book – my first with a proper spine – and nearly all my immediate family were there. My sister had been drafted into driving everyone up to Birmingham. So there they all were, crammed into a row of seats in a bookshop, my dad beaming and craning above the heads of the other punters.

'You were good,' he said afterwards. There was some surprise in his voice. 'The way you dropped your voice for the end of that one poem …'

Mum told me she'd had to lean hard on his elbow during the Q&A section of the event, to stop him asking a question.

The following month he received the news that the cancer had spread to his liver. Three months later he was dead.

When I first started trying to write poems in earnest, I was a young secondary school teacher, struggling with the workload and ill-equipped to support the kids I taught at a Watford comprehensive. I loved the way that poetry didn't have to explain anything – after a day at the chalkface, what a relief it was to sit down and write a statement that didn't 'make sense', that didn't have to explicate or justify its existence. The kind of thinking I could do in a poem seemed comfortable, 'right', 'natural', even. Illogical jumps from topic to topic, the way that sounds repeated, the patterns that poems built up, the way these could lead your train of thought in wholly unexpected directions, the sense that anything and everything could be the subject of a poem; I loved it. I loved obsessing over individual words and their connotations – 'What was the word today?' my beloved would ask after a Saturday spent hunched over my laptop – and how each had its own particular flavour that could alter the poem as a whole. I loved the way you could affect not just a sentence's meaning but the whole poem's according to where you started or ended a line or a stanza.

What I discovered, what I am still exploring, is the peculiar and distinctive way of thinking that poetry requires of us when we write and read it. This is not a new discovery. Paul Valéry writes about exactly this in his essay 'Poetry and Abstract Thought', where he uses a beautiful analogy that likens prose to walking and dancing to poetry – and makes the point that, while poetry uses the same language that we use for everyday purposes, it does so to quite different ends:

> Walking, like prose, has a definite aim [...] The dance is quite another matter. It is, of course, a system of actions; but of actions whose end is in themselves. [...] [H]owever different the dance may be from walking and utilitarian movements, it uses the same organs, the same bones, the same muscles, only differently co-ordinated and aroused.

Dancing – that is, poetry – may well have a destination, but that destination as an objective must take its place alongside its pattern of movements, which are just as significant and meaningful. It's a very different way of moving through and being in the world. It makes you feel and think differently to usual – something it shares with the feral borough.

I think about witches and apparitions on moors and heaths. I think about the mythical beasts that exist in the telling. I think about David Constantine's donkey-headed man and the sounds and smells of the forest spilling in through the Tube doors as they slide open. I think about the lovers in the ash tree and its dead shrew. Poetry is another place where all this could exist; we could all live here, deviants and monsters, cyborgs and chimeras, myths and witches and ghosts. Poetry can hold us all. It is capacious and unfenced. We can be anything there.

I read a Seamus Heaney poem at my dad's funeral, taken from a collection I'd given him as a birthday present. Heaney wrote it in memory of his friend, the film-maker David Hammond. The last line contains an image that I think my dad – a life-long atheist – would've appreciated. The poem's narrator has come to his friend's house, knowing he isn't there. Instead, he finds 'a not unwelcoming / Emptiness, as in a midnight hangar // On an overgrown airfield in late summer.' After the funeral, the blazing summer continued, grass browning, leaves dropping. Dad's decline had been swift and I felt almost embarrassed that I still minded ageing and looking older. There was so much to sort out. My mother was grieving him so hard. The thought that there were now fewer years ahead of me than behind me had me ricocheting off it in a panic. It seemed to be a repetition of the terror I'd felt after Tara died, except that now it was a certainty, rather than some unlucky stroke of chance. Walking the paths around Bush Wood – just as I had after Tara died – the terrors were strongly present: I could get ill, have a heart attack, cancer, be violently assaulted; anything could happen. The world and all its dangers crowded in on me.

But then I noticed a wren singing, or disturbed a wood pigeon, or my eye fell on a late wallflower blooming out of a crevice. Or I passed a dog on a lead dragging its human behind it. The neighbour's cat on the wall. We are all of us in this business of living together, I realised. No one and nothing is exempt – and we will all die. It could have been a despairing thought, but to me that year it was not. If it was sad, then it was also comforting, because it connected me in solidarity with every other living thing.

I walk the track by the playing field once more and pause by this plant with its fern-like leaves, its clusters of umbelliferous flowers in white and pink, amongst the grasshopper-populated grasses, beside the discarded chocolate bar wrapper. To the west, the labyrinth. To the north-east, and close, the forest. Closer still, the heath and the wood at the meeting point of three London boroughs. Overhead, fierce sunsets behind the towers. My body will move through time just like the yarrow, will age and die just like the yarrow. It's mysterious to me and for once I don't think of it anxiously, what time has in store. This is enough. I am here in the world now.

SELECT WORKS CONSULTED

FERAL PIGEON

Hammock, W. G., *Leytonstone and Its History with Especial Reference to the Development of Church Services Therein and a Short Account of Former Residents and Residences & Co.* (London: Batten & Davies, 1904).

Farley, Paul and Michael Symmons Roberts, *Edgelands: Journeys into England's True Wilderness* (London: Vintage, 2012).

Mabey, Richard, *The Unofficial Countryside* (Toller Fratum: Little Toller Books, 2010 [1973]).

Rogers, John, *This Other London: Adventures in the Overlooked City* (London: HarperCollins, 2018). Contains an account of attending an actual 'Beating of the Bounds' ceremony on Lammas land near Leyton marshes, at the time of the Olympic Park development.

ARTIFICIAL TREE

Armstrong, Hannah, 'The Lost Landscapes and Interiorscapes of the Eighteenth-Century Estate: Reconstructing Wanstead House and Its Grounds' (PhD, Birkbeck, University of London, 2017) http://bbktheses.da.ulcc.ac.uk/200/1/ Publicversion-2016ArmstrongHphdBBK.pdf, 14 September 2020.

— *Wanstead House: East London's Lost Palace* (Liverpool: Liverpool University Press, 2022).

Harris, Joseph, *Leighton-Stone-Air, a Poem. Or a Poetical Encomium on the Excellency of Its Soil, Healthy Air, and Beauteous Situation ... Also a Pindarick Ode on Prince Eugene of Savoy. Humbly Dedicated to the Worthy Encouragers of the Latin Boarding-School, Newly Erected in Leighton-Stone ; by the Author J.H.* (London: A. Baldwin, 1702). I am indebted to Hannah Armstrong's scholarship for drawing my attention to this poem.

'Technology - Citytree', http://www.evergen.in/citytree.php, accessed 5 January 2022.

Haraway, Donna, 'The Cyborg Manifesto', *Manifestly Haraway* (Minneapolis & London: University of Minnesota Press, 2016), 5-90.

Wohlleben, Peter, 'Street Kids', *The Hidden Life of Trees - What They Feel, How They Communicate: Discoveries from a Secret World* (London: William Collins, 2017), 169-79.

PRIDE OF LEYTON

'Camellias in Britain - an Informal History', https://www.paramountplants. co.uk/blog/index.php/camellias-in-britain/, accessed 8 January 2021.

Denny, Margaret, 'Naming the Gardenia', *The Scientific Monthly*, 67:1 (1948), 17-22.

For the portrait of Richard Warner, see: Diack Johnstone, H, 'John Hoadly to Richard Warner: A Hitherto Unnoticed (and Mainly Theatrical) Correspondence of the Mid-Eighteenth Century', *Journal for Eighteenth-Century Studies*, 30:1 (2007), 27-54, p 33.

Douglas, J, 'The Carnation and Picotee', *The Garden: An illustrated weekly journal of gardening in all its branches*, 32 (London: W. Robinson, 1887), pp. 102-103

'Gilbert Slater', https://threedecks.org/index.php?display_type=show_ crewman&id=31358 , accessed 8 January 2022.

Harkness, Peter, 'Repeat Flowering Old Roses Part Ii', *Historic Roses*, 11 September 2017 https://historicroses.org/repeat-flowering-old-roses-part-ii-peter-harkness/, accessed 21 April 2021.

'Henry W Headland' (1891) Census return for High Street, Leyton, West Ham, Essex. Public Record Office: Piece 1343, folio 89, p. 14. Available at: http://www.ancestry.co.uk (accessed 8 August 2021).

'Henry W Headland' (1901) Census return for High Road, Leyton, West Ham, Essex. Registration subdistrict North Leyton. Public Record Office: Piece: 1620, folio 23, page 37. Available at: http://www.ancestry.co.uk (accessed 8 January, 2022).

Jarvis, Charles E., Ashley Duval, and Peter R. Crane, 'Gardenia Jasminoides: A Traditional Chinese Dye Plant Becomes a Garden Ornamental in Europe',

Curtis's Botanical Magazine, 31:1 (2014), 80-98.

For a note about the grape imported by Richard Warner, see M.H., 'Catalogue of the Fruits in the Horticultural Society's Garden', *The Gardener's Magazine and Register of Rural and Domestic Improvement*, 3 (1827), 371-74.

Main, James, 'Observations on Chinese Scenery, Plants, and Gardening, Made on a Visit to the City of Canton and Its Environs, in the Years 1793 and 1794; Being an Extract from the Journal of Mr. James Main, Sent Thither by the Late Gilbert Slater, Esq. Of Layton, Essex , to Collect the Double Camellias, & C .', *The Gardener's Magazine and Register of Rural and Domestic Improvement*, 2, (1827), 135-40.

J.M., 'Gilbert Slater, Esq., Late of Low-Layton, Essex', *The Gardener's Magazine and Register of Rural and Domestic Improvement*, 3 (1828), 128.

'National Carnation and Picotee Society, Southern Section', *The Garden: An illustrated weekly journal of gardening in all its branches* (1892), 105.

Sabine, Joseph, 'On the Paeonia Moutan, or Tree Paeony and Its Varieties', *The Gardener's Magazine and Register of Rural and Domestic Improvement*, 2 (1827), 423-24.

Sivanandan, A., 'Catching History on the Wing: Conference Speech', *Race & Class*, 50:3 (2009), 94-98, https://journals.sagepub.com/doi/10.1177/0306396808101186, accessed: 18 December, 2021.

The Gardeners' Chronicle: A Weekly Illustrated Journal of Horticulture and Allied Subjects,
— series 3, 29 (1901).
— series 3, 32 (1902).
— series 3, 34, (1903).

Venison, Tony, 'Tropic of Leytonstone', *Country Life*, 188/44 (1994), 68-71.

ORANGE BONNET

Lister, Arthur and Gulielma Lister, *A Monograph of the Mycetozoa : A Descriptive Catalogue of the Species in the Herbarium of the British Museum*, 2nd ed.

rev. by Gulielma Lister, (London: British Museum, 1911), https://www.biodiversitylibrary.org/item/61303#page/9/mode/1up, accessed 9 August, 2021.

Ramsbottom, J., 'Miss Gulielma Lister', *Nature*, 164: 4159 (1949), 94, doi:10.1038/164094a0, accessed 9 August, 2021.

DOMESTIC SHORT HAIR CAT

Cage, John, *Silence: Lectures and Writings*, (Middletown, Conn.: Wesleyan University Press, 1961).

HAWTHORN

Arnopp, Richard, 'The Owners of Wanstead Park Part 7: 1673-1699', https://wansteadpark.org.uk/history/the-owners-of-wanstead-park-part-7-1673-1699/ , Nov 20, 2012, accessed July 12, 2019.

— 'The Owners of Wanstead Park Part 8: 1699-1750', https://wansteadpark.org.uk/history/the-owners-of-wanstead-park-part-8-1699-1750/ , Nov 20, 2012, accessed July 12, 2019.

— 'The Owners of Wanstead Park Part 10: 1784-1825' , https://wansteadpark.org.uk/history/the-owners-of-wanstead-park-part-10-1784-1824/ , Nov 20, 2012, accessed July 12, 2019.

Claire M Belcher et al., 'Uk Wildfires and Their Climate Challenges: Expert Led Report Prepared for the Third Climate Change Risk Assessment', (Global Systems Institute, University of Exeter, 2021).

Chacko, Roy, 'Two Separate Grass Fires in Wanstead Flats Destroy Three Hectares of Shrubland, *Ilford Recorder*, 11 August 2020, https://www.ilfordrecorder.co.uk/news/grass-fire-spreads-in-wanstead-flats-3266346 , accessed August 12, 2020.

Leyton and Leytonstone Historical Society, https://www.leytonhistorysociety.org.uk , accessed July 11, 2019.

Martin, Fiona and Geoff Sinclair, 'Wanstead Flats: Individual Site Plan', City of London Corporation, 8 January 2020, https://democracy.cityoflondon. gov.uk/documents/s128335/SEF%2003-20%20Wanstead%20Flats%20 ISP%20December%202019%20v4%20FINAL.pdf , accessed 5 July 2021.

'Wanstead Flats Grass Fire Tackled by 200 Firefighters', 15 July 2018, https://www. bbc.co.uk/news/uk-england-44838947, accessed August 12, 2020

SKYLARK

Thomson, Paul, 'Epping Forest - Superintendent's Update for May to June 2020', (City of London Corporation, 2020).

ASH

Edwards, Richard, 'Ash Dieback', https://ltoa.org.uk/281-ash-dieback , accessed 17th November 2021.

Ordnance Survey, 'Essex Lxxiii.Ne', OS 25 inch England and Wales, 1841-1952 (1898 [Revised: 1893 to 1894]).

Porter, Roy, *London: A Social History* (London: Penguin, 1996).

St. John, Allen, 'Bruce Springsteen's Favorite Guitar: The Story Behind One-of-a-Kind Fender', *Rolling Stone* (October 13, 2016), https://www.rollingstone. com/music/music-features/bruce-springsteens-favorite-guitar-the-story-behind-one-of-a-kind-fender-119846/, accessed 7 August 2021.

Westlake, Meryl, 'Ash Dieback: The Devastating Fungus', Royal Botanic Gardens, Kew. https://www.kew.org/read-and-watch/what-is-ash-dieback, accessed 22 August, 2021.

White, Gilbert, 'Letter 28 to the Hon. Daines Barrington', *The Natural History of Selborne* (Ware: Wordsworth Editions, 1996), 227-9.

WHITE-CHEEKED TURACO

Birdlife International, 'Species Factsheet: Tauraco Leucotis', http://datazone.

birdlife.org/species/factsheet/white-cheeked-turaco-tauraco-leucotis, accessed 30 December 2021.

Borges, Jorge Luis and Margarita Guerrero, *The Book of Imaginary Beings*, trans. Norman Thomas Di Giovanni (Harmondsworth: Penguin, 1974).

Harland, Gail, 'The White-Cheeked Turaco', *International Turaco Society*, http://www. turacos.org/whitecheekedextra.htm, accessed 30 December 2021.

HOPS

Drugs and Lactation Database (LactMed) [Internet]. Bethesda (MD): National Library of Medicine (US); 2006-. Hops. [Updated 2021 Feb 15]. Available from: https://www.ncbi.nlm.nih.gov/books/NBK501833/ accessed 30 December 2021.

Walthamstow Beer Project, https://www.walthamstowbeerproject.co.uk/, accessed 30 December 2021.

NOS

Carson, Anne, *Nox*, (New York: New Directions, 2010).

COMMON WOOD PIGEON

Harrap, Simon, *Harrap's Wild Flowers: A Field Guide to the Wild Flowers of Britain and Ireland* (London: Bloomsbury, 2013).

COMMON KESTREL

Hopkins, Gerard Manley, '12 the Windhover: To Christ Our Lord', *Poems of Gerard Manley Hopkins* (London, 1918), 29.

BLACKTHORN

'2137 – Wand: Rod', https://museumofwitchcraftandmagic.co.uk/object/wand-rod/, accessed 15 December 2021.

'2765 – Oil: Phial', https://museumofwitchcraftandmagic.co.uk/object/oil-phial/, accessed 15 December 2021.

Chiej, Roberto, *The Macdonald Encyclopedia of Medicinal Plants*, trans. Sylvia Mulcahy (London, Sydney: Macdonald and Co., 1984), entry 253.

McManus, Damian, *A Guide to Ogam* (Maynooth: An Segart, 1997).

Tongue, R L, 'The Twisty Stick', *Folklore*, 82:3 (1971), 245-46.

Wallis, Jenny and Robert J Blaine, 'Sites, Texts, Contexts and Inscriptions of Meaning: Investigating Pagan "Authenticities" in a Text-Based Society', *The Pomegranate*, 6:2 (2004), 231-52.

RED KITE

Ian M Evans et al., 'The Re-Establishment of Red Kite Breeding Populations in Scotland and England', *British Birds*, 90 (1997), 123-38.

'The "Great" Conjunction of Jupiter and Saturn', https://www.nasa.gov/feature/the-great-conjunction-of-jupiter-and-saturn, accessed 15 December, 2020.

S. R. Wotton et al., 'Breeding Status of the Red Kite Milvus Milvus in Britain in 2000', *Bird Study*, 49:3 (2002), 278-86.

CANALAG

Dee, Tim, *Landfill* (Toller Fratrum: Little Toller Books, 2018).

Del Hoyo, Josep, Elliott, Andy and Christie, David (eds), *Handbook of the Birds of the World*, (Barcelona: Lynx Edicions, 1992-2013).

Fabricius, Eric, 'Interspecific Mate Choice Following Cross-Fostering in a Mixed Colony of Greylag Geese (Anser Anser) and Canada Geese (Branta Canadensis). A Study on Development and Persistence of Species Preferences', *Ethology*, 88:4 (1991), 287-96.

Frank Gill, David Donsker & Pamela Rasmussen (eds), *IOC World Bird List*, 11.1, https://www.worldbirdnames.org/new/classification/ Updated 19-Jan-2021 , accessed 28 January 2021.

Jente Ottenburghs et al., 'Hybridization in Geese: A Review', *Frontiers in Zoology*, 131 (2016), 20.

GREYLAG GOOSE

Delany, Simon, 'Survey of Introduced Geese in Britain, Summer 1991: Provisional Results', (Slimbridge: The Wildfowl and Wetlands Trust, 1992).

COMMON LIME

Couch, Sarah M, 'The Practice of Avenue Planting in the Seventeenth and Eighteenth Centuries', *Garden History*, 20:2 (1992), 173-200.

Evelyn, John, *The Diary of John Evelyn*, (edited by E.S de Beer, (Oxford: Clarendon Press, 2000).

Marks, Jonathan, 'Long Shadow of Linnaeus's Human Taxonomy', *Nature*, 447: 7140 (2007), 28-28.

Notton, David and Christopher Stringer, 'Who Is the Type of Homo Sapiens?', *International Commission on Zoological Nomenclature*, (01/01 2010). Accessed 3 September 2021.

Pigott, Donald, 'The Clones of Common Lime (Tilia X Vulgaris Hayne) Planted in England During the Seventeenth and Eighteenth Centuries', *New Phytologist* (121, 1992), 487- 493.

COMMON BLACK ANT

Sprackland, Jean, 'Aphid Farm', *Green Noise* (London: Jonathan Cape, 2018), 26-7.

LOITERER

'About the Mosquito Alarm', https://mosquitoloiteringsolutions.com/why-mosquito/about-the-mosquito/, accessed 7th January, 2021

Alpers, Paul J, *What Is Pastoral?*, (Chicago: University of Chicago Press, 1996).

Dent, Grace, 'Percy Pigs for Breakfast and Sourdough by Bike: The New

Food World That I Won't Give Up', *The Guardian*, 5 June 2020 https://www.theguardian.com/food/2020/jun/05/percy-pigs-for-breakfast-and-sourdough-by-bike-the-new-food-world-that-i-wont-give-up-grace-dent, accessed 6 June 2020.

Hansard HC Deb. vol. 645 col.s 253-255 number(s), 17th July, 2018, https://www.parliament.uk/ , accessed 20 July 2020.

Ivers, BC, 'Somerset House Fountain Court', *Staging Urban Landscapes : the Activation and Curation of Flexible Public Spaces* (Birkhäuser, 2018), 241-43.

Osley, Richard, 'Mosquito' Alarm at Parliament Hill Lido to Target Young Ears', *Camden New Journal*, 24 April, 2020.

Moore, Rowan, *Slow Burn City: London in the Twenty-First Century* (London: Picador, 2016).

MUNTJAC

Chapman, Norma G, 'History of Introduction of Reeves' Muntjac in Great Britain and Ecological Characteristics Facilitating Expansion of Feral Populations', *European Journal of Wildlife Research*, 67:3 (2021), 33.

BLUEBELL

Barker, Cicely Mary, *Flower Fairies of the Spring* (London: Blackie, 1923).

Grundmann, M. et al, 'Phylogeny and taxonomy of the bluebell genus Hyacinthoides, Asparagaceae [Hyacinthaceae]', *Taxon*, 59 (2010), 68-82.

Ovid, *Metamorphoses*, trans. Mary M. Innes (Harmondsworth: Penguin, 1955).

Rix, Martyn, 'Plate 481. Hyacinthoides non-scripta Hyacinthaceae', *Curtis's Botanical Magazine*, 21 (2004), 20-25.

'Scientists and conservation charities join forces to track Spanish bluebell invasion', 6 April, 2016, https://www.sanger.ac.uk/news/view/scientists-and-conservation-charities-join-forces-track-spanish-bluebell-invasion , accessed 6 October, 2016.

Scott, Carole, 'Clothed in Nature or Nature Clothed: Dress as Metaphor in the

Illustrations of Beatrix Potter and C. M. Barker', *Children's Literature: Annual of The Children's Literature Association and The Modern Language Association Division on Children's Literature*, 22 (1994), 70-89.

SWEET CHESTNUT

Dabydeen, David, 'Blacks and the Polite World of Eighteenth-Century English Art', *Kunapipi*, 6:2 (1984).

Fowler, Corinne, *Green Unpleasant Land* (London: Peepal Tree Press, 2020).

Sen, Paul, 'Tiny finding that opened new frontier', 25 July, 2007, http://news.bbc.co.uk/1/hi/sci/tech/6914175.stm, accessed 10 December 2021.

BOA CONSTRICTOR

Constantine, David, *Selected Poems* (Newcastle upon Tyne: Bloodaxe Books, 1991), p. 146.

Jacob, Gemma, 'Bedbugs', (Transport for London, 2018), https://tfl.gov.uk/corporate/transparency/freedom-of-information/foi-request-detail?referenceId=FOI-2107-1819, accessed 12 July 2021.

Jamie, Kathleen, *Sightlines* (London: Sort Of, 2012).

Sherwood, Harriet, 'Bedbugs Plague Hits British Cities', *The Guardian*, 19 August 2018.

'Snake Used as Face Mask on Bus', https://www.bbc.co.uk/news/uk-england-manchester-54163293 , accessed 10th April 2021.

Transport For London, 'Conditions of Carriage', (2021).

RING-NECKED PARAKEET

Woodward, Ian; Arnold, Richard W; Smith, Neil, *Parrots in the London Area: A London Bird Atlas Supplement* (c.2017).

Fountain, Mark, 'An Immigrant Story', https://www.flocktogether.world/latest/an-immigrant-story , accessed: 19th December, 2021.

O. J. N. Heald et al., 'Understanding the Origins of the Ring-Necked Parakeet in the Uk', *Journal of Zoology*, 312/1 (2020), 1-11.

Reddy, Jini, *Wanderland: A Search for Magic in the Landscape* (London: Bloomsbury, 2020)

LESSER REDPOLL

Woodward, Ian, Arnold, Richard W, Smith, Neil, 'Lesser Redpoll', *The London Bird Atlas*, 16, (London: London Natural History Society and John Beaufoy Publishing, 2017), 356-357.

SWALLOW

Battye, William; Aneja, Viney P and Schlesinger, William H, 'Is nitrogen the next carbon?', *Earth's Future*, 5:9 (2017), 894-904.

Carson, Anne, 'The Glass Essay', *Glass, Irony and God* (New York: New Directions, 1995), 1-38.

Cole, Lucinda, 'Of Mice and Moisture: Rats, Witches, Miasma and Early Modern Theories of Contagion', *Journal for Early Modern Studies*, 10 (2), 2010, pp. 65-84, JSTOR, http://www.jstor.org/stable/23242141, accessed June 15, 2021.

Kaaber, Lars, *Murdering Ministers : A Close Look at Shakespeare's Macbeth in Text, Context and Performance* (Cambridge Scholars Publishing, 2016).

Mellor, Anne K., 'The Baffling Swallow: Gilbert White, Charlotte Smith and the Limits of Natural History', *Nineteenth-Century Contexts*, 31/4 (2009/12/01 2009), 299-309.

Shakespeare, William and Kenneth Muir, *Macbeth* (London: Arden Shakespeare, 1951), 2-190.

Süner, Ahmet, 'Air, Bubble and the Horrid Image: The Representation of Fear and the Supernatural in Macbeth', *Neophilologus*, 103:4 (2019), 591-605.

JERSEY TIGER MOTH

JNCC, 'Conservation status assessment for the species: S6199 – Jersey tiger moth

(Euplagia quadripunctaria) for the 2019 Article 17 reporting under the European Community Directive on the Conservation of Natural Habitats and of Wild Fauna and Flora', (Peterborough: Joint Nature Conservation Committee, 2019), https://jncc.gov.uk/jncc-assets/Art17/S6199-UK-Habitats-Directive-Art17-2019.pdf, accessed 20 August 2020.

SIX-TOED CAT

Hare, David, 'Rowan Williams: God's Boxer', *The Guardian*, 8 July 2011, https://www.theguardian.com/uk/2011/jul/08/rowan-williams-interview-david-hare, accessed 17 January 2022.

Nagel, Thomas, 'What is it Like to Be a Bat?', *The Philosophical Review*, 83 (4), 1974, pp. 435-450.

COMMON WREN

Merleau-Ponty, Maurice, *Phenomenology of Perception*, trans. Colin Smith (London: Routledge, 2002).

YARROW

Heaney, Seamus, ' "The door was open and the house was dark" ', *Human Chain* (London: Faber and Faber, 2010), 82.

Homer, trans. E.V. Rieu, *The Iliad* (Harmondsworth: Penguin, 1950).

Valéry, Paul, 'Poetry and Abstract Thought', in Jackson Mathews (ed.), *The Art of Poetry*, 7 (London: Routledge & Kegan Paul, 1958), 52-81.

ACKNOWLEDGMENTS

Some of the ideas in this book first found expression in academic mode – so thanks again to UEA's Faculty of Arts and Humanities for a studentship and to my PhD supervisors, Denise Riley and David Nowell Smith. Thanks also to the organisers and fellow participants of the following events, where I tried out those ideas: The Annual Meeting of the American Comparative Literature Association, 2017, Universiteit Utrecht; Hybrid Writing: Literary Criticism, Critical Literature, 2016, University of East Anglia.

The Ginkgo Prize and Penned in the Margins commissioned essays to appear on their websites, parts of which are incorporated into *Feral Borough*. Other sections first appeared as intermittent despatches on my website, https://furtive11.wordpress.com.

I couldn't want for a more patient or supportive commissioning editor than Tom Chivers. It's down to his encouragement and enthusiasm that the book even exists. Thank you again and as well to Tom and to Roisin Dunnett for their perceptive editorial work – and to Jo Mortimer for her meticulous proofreading. Jade They and Oliver Barrett perfectly captured the book's feral heart in their artwork.

A huge thank you to my sister, Rhianon Halford, for her kindness and for reading the manuscript and helping me with perspective. Lastly, thank you to Richard Dunn, the 'beloved' I mention throughout, who's borne all the hand-wringing and intense monologuing with such stoic affection. I don't know what I would have done without you, but I wouldn't have been able to write this thing – and so it is, actually, for you, Richard.